THE
13 STEPS TO
RICHES

Featuring
Erik Swanson & Brian Tracy

MASTERMIND
VOLUME 9

HABITUDE
WARRIOR

Including 'The Artiste' Patrick Carney

Copyright © 2023

THE 13 STEPS TO RICHES

All rights reserved. No part of this publication may be reproduced, distributed, or transmitted in any form or by any means, including photocopying, recording, or other electronic or mechanical methods, without the prior written permission of the publisher and Habitude Warrior Int., except in the case of brief quotations embodied in critical reviews and certain other noncommercial uses permitted by copyright law. For permission requests, write to the publisher, addressed "Attention: Permissions Coordinator," at info@beyondpublishing.net.

Permission was granted and approved to use Celebrity Author's testimonials and contributing chapters, quotes and thoughts throughout the book series, but it is understood that this series was not created by or published by the Napoleon Hill Foundation. Quantity sales special discounts are available on quantity purchases by corporations, associations, and others. For details, contact the publisher at the address above.

Orders by U.S. trade bookstores and wholesalers.
Email info@BeyondPublishing.net

Manufactured and printed in the United States of America and distributed globally by Beyond Publishing.

Library of Congress Control Number: 2023902405

ISBN Paperback: 978-1-63792-450-1

ISBN Hardcover: 978-1-63792-453-2

TESTIMONIALS
THE 13 STEPS TO RICHES

"What an honor to collaborate with so many personal development leaders from around the world as we Co-Author together honoring the amazing principles by Napoleon Hill in this new book series, *The 13 Steps to Riches*, by Habitude Warrior and Erik "Mr. Awesome" Swanson. Well done "Mr. Awesome" for putting together such an amazing series. If you want to up-level your life, read every book in this series and learn to apply each of these time tested steps and principles."

Denis Waitley ~ Author of *Psychology of Winning & The NEW Psychology of Winning - Top Qualities of a 21st Century Winner*

"Just as **Think and Grow Rich** reveals the 13 steps to success discovered by Napoleon Hill after interviewing the richest people around the world (and many who considered themselves failures) in the early 1900's, **The 13 Steps to Riches**, produced by Habitude Warrior and Erik Swanson takes a modern look at those same 13 steps. It brings together many of today's personal development leaders to share their stories of how *the 13 Steps to Riches* have created and propelled their own successes. I am honored to participate and share the power of Faith in my life. If you truly want to accelerate reaching the success you deserve, read every volume of *The 13 Steps to Riches*."

Sharon Lechter ~ 5 Time N.Y. Times Best-Selling Author. Author of **Think and Grow Rich** *for Women*, Co-Author of *Exit Rich, Rich Dad Poor Dad, Three Feet from Gold, Outwitting the Devil* and *Success and Something Greater* ~ **SharonLechter.com**

"The most successful book on personal achievement ever written is now being elaborated upon by many of the world's top thought leaders. I'm honored to Co-Author this series on the amazing principles from Napoleon Hill, in *The 13 Steps to Riches,* by Habitude Warrior, Erik "Mr. Awesome" Swanson."

> ***Jim Cathcart*** ~ Best-Selling Author of *Relationship Selling* and *The Acorn Principle,* among many others. Certified Speaking Professional (CSP) and Former President of the National Speakers Association (NSA)

"Some books are written to be read and placed on the shelf. Others are written to transform the reader, as they travel down a path of true transcendence and enlightenment. "*The 13 steps to Riches*" by Habitude Warrior and Erik Swanson is the latter. Profoundly insightful, it revitalizes the techniques and strategies written by Napoleon Hill by applying a modern perspective, and a fearsome collaboration of some of the greatest minds and thought leaders from around the globe. A must read for all of those who seek to break free of their current levels of success, and truly extract the greatness that lies within. It is an honor and a privilege to have been selected to participate, in what is destined to be the next historic chapter in the meteoric rise of many men and women around the world."

> ***Glenn Lundy*** ~ Husband to one, Father to 8, Automotive Industry Expert, Author of "The Morning 5", Creator of the popular morning show "#riseandgrind", and the Founder of "Breakfast With Champions"

"How exciting to team up with the amazing Habitude Warrior community of leaders such as Erik Swanson, Sharon Lechter, John Assaraf, Denis Waitley and so many more transformational and self-help icons to bring you these timeless and proven concepts in the fields of success and wealth. ***The 13 Steps to Riches*** book series will help you reach your dreams and accomplish your goals faster than you have ever experienced before!"

> ***Marie Diamond*** ~ Featured in *The Secret,* Modern Day Spiritual Teacher, Inspirational Speaker, Feng Shui Master

"If you are looking to crystalize your mightiest dream, rekindle your passion, breakthrough limiting beliefs and learn from those who have done exactly what you want to do - read this book! In this transformational masterpiece, ***The 13 Steps to Riches***, self-development guru Erik Swanson has collected the sage wisdom and time tested truths from subject matter experts and amalgamated it into a one-stop-shop resource library that will change your life forever!"

>   **Dan Clark** ~ Speaker Hall of Fame & N.Y. Times Best-Selling Author of *The Art of Significance*

"Life has always been about who you surround yourself with. I am in excellent company with this collaboration from my fellow authors and friends, paying tribute to the life changing principles by Napoleon Hill in this amazing new book series, ***The 13 Steps to Riches***, organized by Habitude Warrior's founder and my dear friend, Erik Swanson. Hill said, 'Your big opportunity may be right where you are now.' This book series is a must-read for anyone who wants to change their life and prosper, starting now."

>   **Alec Stern** ~ America's Startup Success Expert, Co-Founder of Constant Contact

"Finally a book series that encompasses the lessons the world needs to learn and apply, but in our modern day era. As I always teach my students to "Say ***YES***, and then figure out how", I strongly urge you to do the same. Say YES to adding all of these 13 books in ***The 13 Steps to Riches*** book series into your success library and watch both your business as well as your personal life grow as a result."

>   **Loral Langemeier** ~ 5 Time N.Y. Times Best-Selling Author, Featured in *The Secret*, Author of *The Millionaire Maker* and *YES! Energy - The Equation to Do Less, Make More*

"Napoleon Hill had a tremendous impact on my consciousness when I was very young – there were very few books nor the type of trainings that we see today to lead us to success. Whenever you have the opportunity to read and harness *The 13 Steps to Riches* as they are presented in this series, be happy (and thankful) that there were many of us out there applying the principles, testing the teachings, making the mistakes, and now being offered to you in a way that they are clear, simple and concise – with samples and distinctions that will make it easier for you to design a successful life which includes adding value to others, solving world problems, and making the world work for 100% of humanity… Read on… those dreams are about to come true!"

Doria Cordova ~ CEO of Money & You, Excellerated Business School, Global Business Developer, Ambassador of New Education

"Success leaves clues and the Co-Authors in this awesome book series, *The 13 Steps to Riches*, will continue the Napoleon Hill legacy with tools, tips and modern-day principals that greatly expand on the original masterpiece… *Think and Grow Rich*. If you are serious about living your life to the max, get this book series now!"

John Assaraf ~ Chairman & CEO NeuroGym, MrNeuroGym.com, New York Times best-selling author of *Having It All, Innercise,* and *The Answer*. Also featured in *The Secret*

"Over the years, I have been blessed with many rare and amazing opportunities to invest my time and energy. These opportunities require a keen eye and immediate action. This is one of those amazing opportunities for you as a reader! I highly recommend you pick up every book in this series of *The 13 Steps to Riches* by Habitude Warrior and Erik Swanson! Learn from modern day leaders who have embraced the lessons from the great Napoleon Hill in his classic book from 1937, *Think and Grow Rich.*"

Kevin Harrington ~ Original "Shark" on *Shark Tank*, Creator of the Infomercial, Pioneer of the *As Seen on TV* brand, Co-Author of *Mentor to Millions*

"When you begin your journey, you will quickly learn of the importance of the first step of **The 13 Steps To Riches**. A burning desire is the start of all worthwhile achievements. Erik 'Mr. Awesome' Swanson's newest book series contains a wealth of assistance to make your journey both successful and enjoyable. Start today... because tomorrow is not guaranteed on your calendar."

> **Don Green** ~ 45 Years of Banking, Finance & Entrepreneurship, Best-Selling Author of *Everything I know About Success I Learned From Napoleon Hill* & *Napoleon Hill My Mentor: Timeless Principles to Take Your Success to the Next Level* & *Your Millionaire Mindset*

Our minds become magnetized with the dominating thoughts we hold in our minds and these magnets attract to us the forces, the people, the circumstances of life which harmonize with the nature of our dominating thoughts.

(Napoleon Hill)

Global Speakers Mastermind & Habitude Warrior Masterminds

Join us and become a member of our tribe! Our Global Speakers Mastermind is a virtual group of amazing thinkers and leaders who meet twice a month. Sessions are designed to be 'to the point' and focused, while sharing fantastic techniques to grown your mindset as well as your pocket books. We also include famous guest speaker spots for our private Masterclasses. We also designate certain sessions for our members to mastermind with each other & counsel on the topics discussed in our previous Masterclasses. It's time for you to join a tribe who truly cares about **YOU** and your future and start surrounding yourself with the famous leaders and mentors of our time. It is time for you to up-level your life, businesses, and relationships.

For more information to check out our Masterminds:
Team@HabitudeWarrior.com
www.DecideToBeAwesome.com

FREE GIFT!
GRAB YOUR SPECIAL
& AWESOME FREE GIFT!

We have a very special gift for those who want to surround themselves with a tribe of people creating magic in supporting each other and their growth in their personal and professional lives! It's time for you to be up-leveled in such a fantastic way! You deserve to reward yourself and join us. "NDSO!" No Drama - Serve Others!

Visit the QR code link above to get your FREE GIFT!
www.RideAlongGuestPass.com

NAPOLEON HILL

I would like to personally acknowledge and thank the one and only Napoleon Hill for his work, dedication, and most importantly believing in himself. His unwavering belief in himself, whether he realized this or not, had been passed down from generation to generation to millions and millions of individuals across this planet including me!

I'm sure, at first, as many of us experience throughout our lives as well, he most likely had his doubts. Think about it. Being offered to work for Andrew Carnegie for a full 20 years with zero pay and no guarantee of success had to be a daunting decision. But, I thank you for making that decision years and years ago. It paved the path for countless many who have trusted in themselves and found success in their own rights. You gave us all hope, desire, and faith to bank on the most important energy in the world - ourselves!

For this, I thank you Sir, from the bottom of my heart and the top of all of our bank accounts. Let us all follow *The 13 Steps to Riches* and prosper in so many areas of our lives.

~ Erik "Mr. Awesome" Swanson

13 Time #1 Best-Selling Author & Student of Napoleon Hill Philosophies

Lance Cpl. Rylee J. McCollum, 20

It is our distinct honor to dedicate each one of *The 13 Steps to Riches* book volumes to each of the 13 United States Service Members who courageously lost their lives in Kabul in August, 2021. Your honor, dignity, and strength will always be cherished and remembered.

~ Habitude Warrior Team

Lance Cpl. Rylee J. McCollum, 20, of Jackson, Wyoming, a rifleman.

His awards and decorations include the National Defense Service Medal and Global War on Terrorism Service Medal. Additional awards pending approval may include Purple Heart, Combat Action Ribbon and Sea Service Deployment Ribbon. We honor you and thank you for your ultimate sacrifice!

THE 13 STEPS TO RICHES FEATURING:

DENIS WAITLEY ~ Author of *Psychology of Winning & The NEW Psychology of Winning - Top Qualities of a 21st Century Winner*, NASA's Performance Coach, Featured in *The Secret* ~ www.DenisWaitley.com

SHARON LECHTER ~ 5 Time N.Y. Times Best-Selling Author. Author of *Think and Grow Rich for Women*, Co-Author of *Exit Rich, Rich Dad Poor Dad, Three Feet from Gold, Outwitting the Devil* and *Success and Something Greater* ~ www.SharonLechter.com

JIM CATHCART~ Best-Selling Author of *Relationship Selling* and *The Acorn Principle,* among many others. Certified Speaking Professional (CSP) and Former President of the National Speakers Association (NSA) ~ www.Cathcart.com

MICHAEL E. GERBER ~ New York Times Bestseller of the mega best selling theory for over two consecutive decades... E-Myth books.
~ www.MichaelEGerberCompanies.com

GLENN LUNDY ~ Husband to one, Father to 8, Automotive Industry Expert, Author of "The Morning 5", Creator of the popular morning show "#riseandgrind", and the Founder of "Breakfast With Champions"
~ www.GlennLundy.com

MARIE DIAMOND ~ Featured in *The Secret*, Modern Day Spiritual Teacher, Inspirational Speaker, Feng Shui Master ~ www.MarieDiamond.com

DAN CLARK ~ Award Winning Speaker, Speaker Hall of Fame, N.Y. Times Best-Selling Author of *The Art of Significance* ~ www.DanClark.com

ALEC STERN ~ America's Startup Success Expert, Co-Founder of Constant Contact, Speaker, Mentor, Investor ~ www.AlecSpeaks.com

ERIK SWANSON ~ 13 Time #1 International Best-Selling Author, Award Winning Speaker, Featured on Tedx Talks and Amazon Prime TV. Founder & CEO of the Habitude Warrior Brand ~ www.SpeakerErikSwanson.com

LORAL LANGEMEIER ~ 5 Time N.Y. Times Best-Selling Author, Featured in *The Secret*, Author of *The Millionaire Maker* and *YES! Energy - The Equation to Do Less, Make More* ~ www.LoralLangemeier.com

DORIA CORDOVA ~ CEO of Money & You, Excellerated Business School, Global Business Developer, Ambassador of New Education ~ www.FridaysWithDoria.com

JOHN ASSARAF ~ Chairman & CEO NeuroGym, MrNeuroGym.com, N. Y. Times best-selling author of *Having It All*, *Innercise*, and *The Answer*. Also featured in *The Secret* ~ www.JohnAssaraf.com

KEVIN HARRINGTON ~ Original "Shark" on the hit TV show *Shark Tank*, Creator of the Infomercial, Pioneer of the *As Seen on TV* brand, Co-Author of *Mentor to Millions* ~ www.KevinHarrington.TV

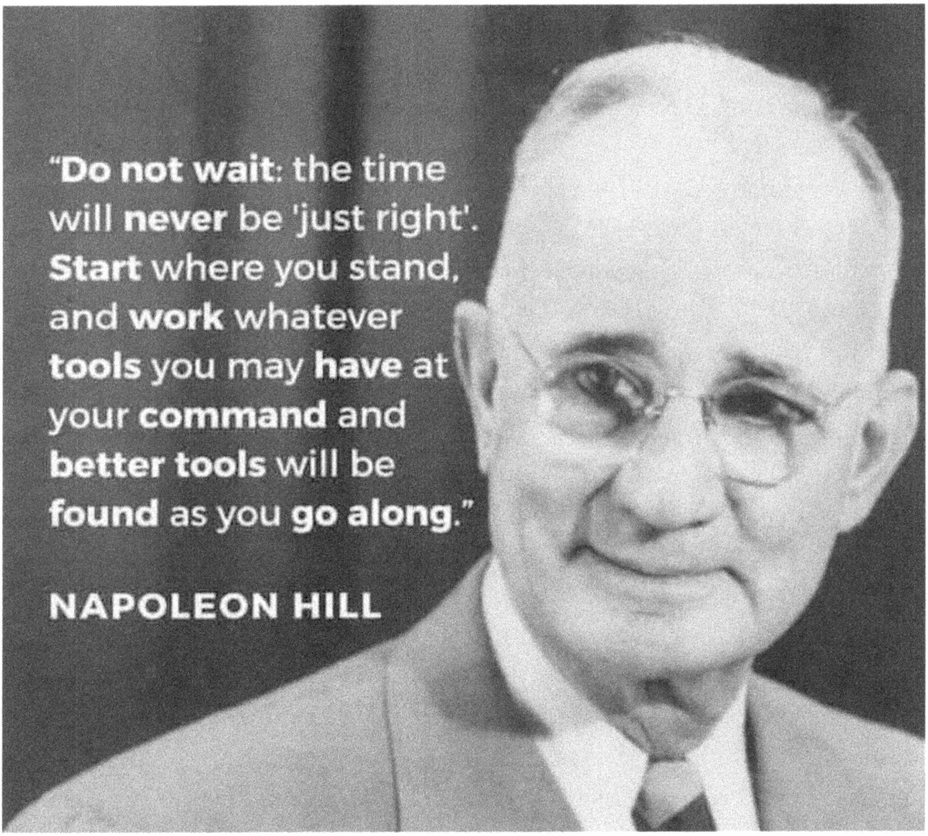

"**Do not wait**: the time will **never** be 'just right'. **Start** where you stand, and **work** whatever **tools** you may **have** at your **command** and **better tools** will be **found** as you **go along**."

NAPOLEON HILL

CONTENTS

Testimonials	What Others Are Saying	5
Acknowledgment	To Napoleon Hill	13
Dedication	Lance Cpl. Rylee J. McCollum	15
Celebrity Authors	The 13 Featured Celebrity Authors	17
Introduction	By Don Green	23
Brian Tracy	The Power Of Masterminds	25
Erik Swanson	Master Your Mind In A True Mastermind	29
Patrick Carney	The Mastermind Mindset	34
Jon Kovach Jr.	Accelerated Results In The Spirit Of Harmony	43
Amado Hernandez	Control Your Mind	55
Angelika Ullsperger	Sharing Infinite Knowledge	62
Anthony M. Criniti	Wisely Collect Your Collective Mind	67
Barry Bevier	The Power Of The Mastermind — The Hot Seat	73
Bonnie Lierse	Powerful Masterminds On Steroids	79
Brian Schulman	Together We Do	86
Candace & David Rose	Stream of Power	94
Corey Poirier	The Mastermind	96
Deb Scott	Power Of The Mastermind: The Driving Force	101
Dori Ray	Power On Purpose	107
Elaine Sugimura	Masterminding Your Way To The Pinnacle!	109
Elizabeth Anne Walker	The Driving Force Behind A True Mastermind	115
Erin Ley	Teamwork Makes The Dream Work	121
Fatima Hurd	Master The Mind	127
Frankie Fegurgur	May I Borrow Your Brain?	132
Fred Moskowitz	Harnessing The Power Of The People Around You	138
Gina Bacalski	My First Time	145
Griselda Beck	Expand Your Mind, Accelerate Your Results!	152
Jason Curtis	Knowledge, Effort, & Opportunity	157
Jeffrey Levine	True Power Of The Mastermind	159
Lacey & Adam Platt	Surround Yourself With Amazing People & My First Mastermind	164
Louisa Jovanovich	Bringing Out The Beauty In You	170

Lynda Sunshine West	Master What?	176
Maris Segal & Ken Ashby	Converting Energy Into What Matters With Masterminds	181
Mel Mason	Mastermind Your Way Toward Anything	187
Miatta Hampton	Iron Sharpens Iron	193
Michael D. Butler	The Mastermind Evolution	198
Michelle Cameron Coulter & Al Coulter	Further Together	203
Michelle Mras	The Multiplier Of Abundance	208
Mickey Stewart	Angels In My Attic	213
Natalie Susi	Mastermind Magic	219
Nita Patel	The Secret Mastermind	224
Olga Geidane	Definite Purpose Achieved In A Mastermind	230
Paul Capozio	Two Minds Can Create A Third	231
Phillip McClure	Making A Mastermind	233
Robyn Scott	Master Your Mind!	238
Shannon Whittington	Becoming A Mastermind	244
Soraiya Vasanji	Sisterhoods Or Masterminds Or Both	250
Stacey Ross Cohen	Tap Into The Collective Power Of The Mastermind	257
Teresa Cundiff	How Many Masterminds Are You In?	264
Vera Thomas	Great Minds	270
Yuri Choi	Power Of The Mastermind	277

INTRODUCTION

by Don Green

ERIK SWANSON & DON GREEN

Once you give yourself the gift of reading Erik Swanson's newest book series, ***The 13 Steps to Riches***, you are sure to realize why he has earned his nickname, *"Mr. Awesome."* Readers usually read books for two reasons – they want to be entertained or they want to improve their knowledge in a certain subject. Mr. Awesome's new book series will help you do both.

I urge you to not only read this great book series in its entirety, but also apply the principles held within into your our life. Use the experience Erik Swanson has gained to reach your own level of success. I highly encourage you to invest in yourself by reading self-help materials, such as *The 13 Steps to Riches*, and I truly know you will discover that it will be one of the best investments you could ever make.

Don Green
Executive Director and CEO
The Napoleon Hill Foundation

Brian Tracy

THE POWER OF MASTERMINDS

Greetings! You have the opportunity now to dramatically increase your ability to earn and keep more money than you ever thought possible.

The richest and most influential people in America and probably the world have all discovered the incredible power of the "Mastermind." In interviewing wealthy people, they all recall that the turning point in their road to great success and achievement was when they formed one or more Masterminds.

Each rich person recalls the "turning point" in their life and fortunes. It was the same for all of them. It was when they started to cooperate and work with other successful people.

Many people struggled for years until that magical turning point when they met and began to share ideas with other successful people. Suddenly they were able to tap into the knowledge, experience, and skills of others. In almost no time, their ability to move ahead doubled or tripled—almost overnight.

The key to forming Masterminds is to look around yourself for one or more successful people and then determine how you can help them.

The key to tapping into the "Mastermind Principle" is to look for ways to "Give" before you get. The law of "sowing and reaping" says, "whatsoever ye sow, that also shall ye reap." This is a universal principle that works 100% of the time.

You have complete control over your future and your success without limit. But remember, the only part of this universal law you can control is the "putting in." The riches and rewards will come to you automatically, by "Law," not by chance.

From this day forward, look for ways to put in, to give of yourself. The riches and rewards will come to you faster and greater than you ever thought possible. Go for it!

BRIAN TRACY

Brian Tracy is Chairman and CEO of Brian Tracy International, a company specializing in the training and development of individuals and organizations. Brian's goal is to help you achieve your personal and business goals faster and easier than you ever imagined.

Brian Tracy has consulted for more than 1,000 companies and addressed more than 5,000,000 people in 5,000 talks and seminars throughout the US, Canada and 70 other countries worldwide. As a Keynote speaker and seminar leader, he addresses more than 250,000 people each year.

He has studied, researched, written and spoken for 30 years in the fields of economics, history, business, philosophy and psychology. He is the top selling author of over 70 books that have been translated into dozens of languages.

He has written and produced more than 300 audio and video learning programs, including the worldwide, best-selling Psychology of Achievement, which has been translated into more than 28 languages.

He speaks to corporate and public audiences on the subjects of Personal and Professional Development, including the executives and staff of many of America's largest corporations. His exciting talks and seminars on Leadership, Selling, Self-Esteem, Goals, Strategy, Creativity and Success Psychology bring about immediate changes and long-term results. Brian Tracy is the recipient of many awards including The Habitude Warrior Lifetime Achievement Award.

He has traveled and worked in over 107 countries on six continents, and speaks four languages. Brian is happily married and has four children. He is active in community and national affairs, and is the President of three companies headquartered in Solana Beach, California.

www.BrianTracy.com

Erik "Mr. Awesome" Swanson

MASTER YOUR MIND IN A TRUE MASTERMIND

Let me just start out by saying that I had absolutely no idea what a mastermind really was. Even though I had read and studied Napoleon Hill's work for years upon years, I never grasped the true definition or reasoning behind masterminds until it landed right at my feet.

I had always thought it was one of those woo-woo kinds of mystical things people did. But, to my surprise, it's one of the most important and vital keys to my success and it can also be one of yours.

Getting Started

As I mentioned, the concept of masterminds literally fell into my lap one day. It was a number of years ago when I was conducting one of our Habitude Warrior Global Speakers Conferences. We had close to 1,000 people in attendance virtually on the summit that day. We had so many amazing, famous speakers throughout my summit.

One of the amazing speakers was my close and great friend, Don Green! Don is the President of the Napoleon Hill Foundation. What an amazing human he is! If you ever get a chance to meet him or even simply sit in a room with him, make sure you have your journal and a pen to take as many notes as you possibly can. He will change your life if you allow him to. I owe so much of my success to him. Thank you, Don!

Having Don Green on my summit created a magical moment when I interviewed him about the importance of Napoleon Hill's work. The subject of masterminds came up in the interview. It was super clear to me that our audience was very intrigued and interested in learning more about them. In fact, when we were diving into the Q&A portion of the interview, many of my guests and students raised their hands to ask more about masterminds. One guest even asked me if we provided masterminds to my students. I learned a great technique from my main mentor, Brian Tracy. He taught me to always answer the word 'yes' and then figure out how to provide it the solution. I did just that, and our Habitude Warrior Mastermind was born right then and there!

Say Yes To Others By Saying Yes To Yourself

This is such an important concept to learn and live by. By saying yes to yourself, you give yourself permission to learn and grow. You also give permission to others to learn and grow with you. If you think about it, had you not said yes to yourself in the first place, the magic of what you created would never have been born.

Get Picked For Every Sport

Remember when you were growing up in grade school? I don't know about you, but I was never the most athletic kid in school. Because of this, I would never get picked first for any sport. In fact, I was only picked because there was no one left to pick. You may be wondering why I'm talking about sports right now. The reasoning is that since joining and creating masterminds, I have noticed that everyone is picked! A true, and amazing mastermind, if run correctly, will give everyone in the group equal attention. You will feel part of the in-crowd right from the start. We don't play favorites. We play equally and pour into each mastermind member to allow them to literally feel like they are family. They are.

Join a team who will be there for you through thick and thin. A true mastermind delivers results to everyone in the group. One of the organizer's goals is to make sure every member is 'up-leveling' to that next level of success. This is one of our visions and mottos in the Habitude Warrior Mastermind.

Surround Yourself With Winners

When you join a mastermind, one of the most vital traits is that you are joining a team of winners. It is said that we are the culmination of the books we read and the people we surround ourselves with. By surrounding yourself, on a consistent basis, with the right people can serve to be one of the best things you can possibly do for your business, career, and personal life!

Allow your fellow mastermind members to become your cheerleader. In this day and age, we all need people to support us and cheer us on. Too often, we find ourselves listening and watching negative news and allowing that to seep into our consciousness and, even worse, our subconscious. It's time for you to take charge of your life. But don't do it alone! Another saying tells us that if we want to go fast, go alone. But, if you want to go far, go with a team. Find and go with your mastermind team!

A True Mastermind

So, what is an actual mastermind, and how can it help you? A true mastermind is a group that meets on a regular basis, either in person or virtually. Each meeting is run by an organizer. Each meeting's purpose is to assist each member, either directly or by what's called borrowed benefits, in growing in a certain and specific subject. Although masterminds differ, each meeting typically invites one to three members to sit in what's called the 'hot seat' or 'opportunity chair.' This is their opportunity to ask the group for their support and assistance in a certain subject or challenge they may be having. All members are responsible for giving counsel, rather than opinions, on what the hot seat member should tackle next to resolve the challenge. Each counsel should be based on the member's experience. The borrowed benefits are magically developed by all members taking advantage of learning the principles counseled on even though they were technically not in the opportunity chair. Win, Win, Win!

Master Your Mind

One of the best gifts you can give yourself in this world is to master your mind. In other words, being clear in your life's purpose is vital to a beautiful experience as a human being. A great way to do this more quickly is to join a team of individuals with a common goal, direction, and purpose. Join a mastermind today! In fact, I would like to personally invite you to join my mastermind and allow your life to flourish as you have never seen it flourish before. Allow my team and me to introduce you to members who will become your allies to your success. Our members are cheerleaders waiting to assist you in your habits, attitudes, and business development. Don't go alone; go with a team who will support you in every step you make!

To be invited to meet all of us and check our masterminds, please visit www.RideAlongGuestPass.com and fill our the quick name and email for a direct invite. We look forward to meeting you and growing with you. Erik "Mr. Awesome" Swanson

ERIK SWANSON

About Erik "Mr. Awesome" Swanson: As an Award-Winning International Keynote Speaker and 13 Time #1 Best-Selling Author, Erik "Mr. Awesome" Swanson is in great demand around the world! He speaks to an average of more than one million people per year. He can be seen on Amazon Prime TV in the very popular show *SpeakUP TV*. Mr. Swanson has the honor to have been invited to speak at many universities, such as the University of California (UCSD), Cal State University, University of Southern California (USC), Grand Canyon University (GCU), and the Business and Entrepreneurial School of Harvard University. He is also a Faculty Member of CEO Space International and is a recurring keynoter at Vistage Executive Coaching. Erik also joins the Ted Talk Family with his latest TEDx speech called *"A Dose of Awesome."*

Erik got his start in the self-development world by mentoring directly under the famous Brian Tracy. Quickly climbing to become the top trainer around the world from a group of over 250 hand-picked trainers, Erik started to surround himself with the best of the best and soon started to be invited to speak on stages alongside such greats as Jim Rohn, Bob Proctor, Les Brown, Sharon Lechter, Jack Canfield, and Joe Dispenza... just to name a few. Erik has created and developed the super-popular Habitude Warrior Conference, which has a two-year waiting list and includes 33 top-named speakers worldwide. It is a 'Ted Talk' style event that has quickly climbed to one of the top 10 events not to miss in the United States! He is the creator, founder, and CEO of the Habitude Warrior Mastermind and Global Speakers Mastermind. His motto is clear... "NDSO!": No Drama – Serve Others!

Author's Website: *www.SpeakerErikSwanson.com*
Book Series Website & Author's Bio: *www.The13StepsToRiches.com*

Patrick Carney

THE MASTERMIND MINDSET

"The starting point of all achievement is desire."
~ Napoleon Hill

It is well known that the origin of the term Mastermind is attributed to author Napoleon Hill. Hill defined a Mastermind to be "created through harmony of purpose and effort, between two or more people." In his Law of Success course, Hill said, "Success in this world is always a matter of individual effort, yet you will only be deceiving yourself if you believe that you can succeed without the cooperation of other people." I believe that it takes a network like a Mastermind to nurture a dream. By being around people that can work with you to overcome your challenges, you can create a more fulfilling life.

The origin of a Mastermind group goes as far back as Benjamin Franklin, who used a similar group process, he called a Junto. Franklin said in his autobiography, "I had formed most of my ingenious acquaintances into a club for mutual improvement." Franklin knew that a successful leader is not the head of a team, company, or country but rather the heart of the team, company, or country.

Masterminds are so successful because today's modern communication is fractured and fragmented and does not move in a straight line. Thus, there must be a willingness to surrender to the unanticipated possibilities of the ideas as they unfold. The members of the Mastermind guide you through these infinite possibilities.

The challenge for me currently is that many events are labeled as Masterminds, though they do not include the heart of a true Mastermind, the Hot Seat process. These events generally have speakers on stage preaching their expertise to the participants rather than having them involved in the conversation. When that interaction is eliminated, the growth potential is dramatically reduced.

I've seen people call educational gatherings "Masterminds," investment groups where individuals train Masterminds, consultants who call their meeting "Masterminds," and tech group trainings called "Masterminds."

These may be valuable informational meetings; however, as per the training of Napoleon Hill, they are not true Masterminds. Prior to joining a group, it is vital that one interview the facilitator to make sure they are signing up for a true Mastermind and sit in on a meeting as a guest to listen and observe for the "Hot Seat" process.

The most successful Mastermind groups are small groups of like-minded, successful individuals who meet weekly to support each other's growth. As the group comes together, knowledge is gained when the goals of each member are uniquely explored. This involvement as a member of a Mastermind group creates an opportunity for you to realize that you are willing and committed to becoming more than you ever imagined as a person in business and the world. What I have learned as a weekly Mastermind facilitator is that the common denominator for each member is the acceptance of responsibility for supporting, advising, and challenging other members in pursuit of their individual goals.

An enormous part of improving one's mental and emotional well-being is the connection with others and with a power greater than oneself. Life is a team sport. We were not put on this earth to go it alone. Sometimes miracles come from brilliant, heart-centered people meeting together on a weekly basis that can reinvent lives in a profound way.

The word Mastermind first appeared in the late 17th century. It was described as a person with an outstanding or commanding mind or intellect. Today we understand a Mastermind to be a group that should attract people of brilliant intellect who inspire and motivate each other. Within the group, they exchange personal expertise that can be of value to all members. One's true knowledge comes from our life experiences. Yet, as we gather experience and knowledge, interaction with mentors enhances the learning experience.

One of the remarkable things about being involved with a Mastermind is that unique individuals will join the group and make such a wonderful impact on your life. You will be forever challenged to remember what life was like without them. As the group evolves and member change, those experiences, and insights shared together remain. Conversations and insights shared with past members continue to be relevant and impactful.

What I've learned over the years is that Masterminds are about creating abundance through team effort. The ability to create abundant success in the next 5 to 10 years is affected by the mindset of the people with whom you collaborate. The ability to create fulfillment in the next 5 to 10 years is affected by the fulfillment level of those with whom you collaborate. You will rise or lower yourself to the level of the average of the five people you associate with the most.

When we decided to create a Mastermind Group, we asked ourselves, what was our desire? One of the initial agreements was accountability. The following is a list of attributes that we have determined to contribute to the success of a Mastermind Group.

Established Rules of the Game Similar Vision
    Synergy
    Win Win Win Opportunities

Out-of-the-Box Thinking
An Entrepreneurial Spirit
Being in Integrity
Take Purposeful Action
Have Inspired Creativity
Coachable Members

The amazing benefits of being in a Mastermind are ongoing. Powerful individuals have dedicated themselves to supporting, challenging, cheering you on, and inspiring you to achieve your goals. The group's interest and attention to your goals provide a subtle yet powerful incentive for accountability. The group's individual perspectives, experiences, and wisdom are compounded on your behalf, providing a cooperation well beyond that of everyone. The group's non-judgmental support encourages you to share your fears and dreams openly, getting them out into the open where they can be nurtured effectively.

The magic word which describes the real power known to the mind is the word 'choice.' Every move we make is done by choice. When you make a choice, like joining or forming a Mastermind group, you open the way to results. You must maintain a state of gratitude and awe! Gratitude is the surest way to stop the inner dialogue that keeps us from joy, success, and our divine Source. At the same time, be mindful of negative self-talk. It is, after all, a conversation with the Universe.

A benefit that surprises many members is the opportunity to release versions of yourself you created just to survive. Every thought we think is creating our futures. In a Mastermind, you have a group of individuals helping you format the best outcomes for that future. Diversity is a fact in a Mastermind. Equity is a choice and inclusion, an action. Belonging becomes an outcome. Ultimately, the timeline forever shifts in your favor.

If we believe in the Laws of the Universe, nothing is accidental. We don't meet people in a Mastermind by accident. They are meant to cross our paths and teach us a lesson about life, business, or relationships. In a mastermind group, we are blessed to surround ourselves with individuals who talk about visions and ideas, not other people. A grateful heart in a Mastermind setting is a magnet for miracles.

When one joins a Mastermind group, they are making a commitment to grow. As Buckminster Fuller once said: "The best way to predict the future is to design it." No Mastermind group will function for long if people are unwilling to commit to the group. Commitment comes in two forms: commitment to showing up for every meeting without excuse or justification and commitment to participating in the mastermind group process. Commitment is essential to give and receive the most benefit from the group.

We all have a past; we've all made choices that we may regret or wish to redo. None of us are infallible. However, in a Mastermind, there is an opportunity for a fresh start every week and to be a better person than we were the week before. In a group setting, there is subtle accountability where other members hold you to a higher standard. I believe we are infinite souls living in a world of infinite possibilities. Our future is limitless.

As a group, we maintain a clear purpose for our meetings: contributing ideas and support and keeping each other on target towards our own goals. Each week one member participates in the Hot Seat process, and others share ideas and experiences that will take him/her to the next level. During that week, members follow up with promises made. The strongest value a member gets out of being in a group is the chance to be in the Hot Seat.

The Hot Seat is a treasured time in a Mastermind meeting where one receives feedback and advice from others in the room. In my Mastermind, we designate 1 hour and 15 minutes of a spotlight on your business—the good, the bad, and the ugly. It is amazing how much can come from a time in the Hot Seat. Think about a dozen fresh eyes looking at your business to question and validate your choices and goals and force you to think, prioritize and act.

When each member gets the opportunity to bring their newest idea or project to the group, it forces them to gain clarity about what assistance they are truly asking for. In my Mastermind, members have fifteen minutes to present their ask, idea, project, or question. The key is to know what help one needs and to be precise when articulating it to the group. There might be a challenge you would like the group to explore. Are there things in place that you have already attempted or rabbit holes you would like the group to ignore? If a creative idea is good enough, it will haunt you till you bring it to fruition. When that happens, it's a magical team moment.

The true magic happens when the members brainstorm in the Hot Seat process around a project, question, book, product, or marketing idea. Brainstorming brings vast amounts of creativity to the process. The person in the Hot Seat walks away from the meeting with renewed energy, unique ideas, and referrals to individuals who will help with the process and solutions they should implement over the next few weeks. This process is the key factor that motivates individuals to join mastermind groups and is the reason I have been involved for so many years.

Through the good times, the challenging times, and worse, as members of a Mastermind, we are always together as a team. In life, often more importance is given to the "where" rather than "with whom." Never belittle what you can do with your team. A Mastermind has enabled so many individuals to love their life.

One of my passions is a deep commitment and true understanding of the Mastermind process. My desire is to hear individuals' ideas or challenges and assist in creating a clearer path for them to prosper creatively in wisdom, finance, and spirit. Every excuse one uses not to join a Mastermind is the same reason someone is using to achieve their dreams. Having supportive partners can significantly impact your life in a positive way.

We are forever changing and growing. One's ability to see beauty and possibility is proportionate to the level at which one embraces gratitude. I'm in gratitude every day. My days have been an endless dance of miracles and synchronicities since I started the Mastermind. My journey is not the same as yours; however, if we meet on the Mastermind path, may we lift and encourage each other. The world has enough critics already. While so many quietly live their day-to-day routines, those in a Mastermind are blessed to create and change lives.

PATRICK CARNEY

About Patrick Carney: Patrick Carney the Artiste, is an indomitable spirit who has shared his creative talent with the world in ways that are sometimes beyond measure. No one captures the 'Essence of Women,' the aura of their souls, the contours of their brilliance in the way this artist can. Carney captures the legacy that these women leave as footsteps on this earth.

While attending the School of Visual Arts in New York City, Patrick Carney had the privilege to study with Chuck Close, Marge Anderson, Robert Israel, Burne Hogarth and Milton Glaser; each of these teachers having a profound impact on his life.

As a youth he read voraciously – searching for answers which led to more questions. While pursuing studies at Buffalo State, he worked as a specialist in media at the Communications Center. Later he was named the Art Director of the Lafayette Community Center where he taught art to inner city children. For a time he traveled throughout the NY State as an Artist in Residence at underprivileged high schools as a representative of the Arts Council, and volunteered as a art teacher in the state prison system, believing that it was his obligation to give back and "Pass On" his given talents.

Starting in 1964 in NY's West Village, Mr. Carney dedicated his time to drawing and painting the world of rock n' roll music, it's passion and creativity caught in real time forever. He traveled throughout the US attending rock concerts and painted whatever star excited him – and thus his work is a varied series of welcome surprises.

Hanging out at what he calls "the corner of Art and Soul," the Artiste Patrick Carney creates the images of your youth, capturing on canvas the music you grew up with.

Not only are Patrick Carney's Acrylics and Pen & Inks purchased by collectors all over the world, his paintings are displayed in the personal collections of such luminaries as Dick Clark, John Lennon, Bob Dylan, Stevie Nicks, Bruce Springsteen, JD Souther, Tom Russell, Judy Collins, Al Kooper, Pete Seeger, Sharon Lechter, Erik Swanson and Kevin Harrington.

Book Series Website & Author's Bio: *www.The13StepsToRiches.com*

Jon Kovach Jr.

ACCELERATED RESULTS IN THE SPIRIT OF HARMONY

After grabbing my pen beneath my desk, I had just put in my 2-week notice. I was in a comfortable salaried position. Many of my marketing and public relations peers would have said I was absolutely crazy for walking away from such a promising corporate career choice. I had a career with paved roads to success already set for the next ten years of my life—salary, pensions, retirement funds, and rubbing shoulders with one of the most successful entrepreneurs in Utah and in commercial real estate private brokerage.

While retrieving my fallen pen beneath my desk, I had an epiphany: I gasped out from my inner subconscious and said, "I wish I could hide under here (my desk) all day." I immediately knew I was working a great job with great people on an excellent track for success, but all were not aligned with whom I wanted to become and what impact I would make in the world. I knew deep down that I was meant for something else. An athlete turned entrepreneur; I had grander visions for my future. The publicist and media assistant weren't on that path. The next step was the boldest move I've ever made in my career. I used that same pen to author the letter to my supervisor that I would be resigning.

Without going anywhere or having another job lined up, I had one option—a mastermind. Weeks earlier to this epiphany, I stumbled upon a small entrepreneurial mastermind group held in a small board room in Salt Lake City. I quickly learned that a mastermind was where motivated people gathered to serve each other in finding solutions to their most significant challenges. I was filled with motivation, desire, determination, and accountability as I soaked up every second of the energy gleaned from this environment for success. There indeed, was nothing like it. Of all my school projects, team meetings, award-winning PR campaigns, and meetings, nothing matched the quality and value that was magnified in the environment of a mastermind group. I quickly grew obsessed with this procedure and methodology. But this mastermind had one catch, it wasn't free.

The other business owners and mastermind members loved my enthusiasm and desire to serve. I was told that the room was smarter, happier, and more resourceful when I was in attendance. They encouraged me to do whatever I could to continue to meet with them each week. There were four sessions per month (one per week), and it cost about $500 to maintain a seat at the table and be a qualified member of this mastermind. Not only did I not have $500 to spare each month, but I just wrote my letter of resignation from my salaried job.

This mastermind was the greatest environment I had ever experienced. I valued its production over any university course, workshop, or specialized training I had ever received. I knew I needed to be in that room, just like the infamous Aaron Burr portrayed in the very popular Broadway Musical Hamilton, who knew that the making of policies that shaped the United States of America was to be in the room with the playmakers— George Washington, Thomas Jefferson, Samuel Adams, and his arch nemesis, Alexander Hamilton. His song "In The Room Where It Happens" highlights the same inspiration I felt I had to do anything I could to remain in that mastermind boardroom.

I quickly picked up side jobs driving for Uber (making almost $400 per week), delivering pizzas and food (earning tips), contracting work for clients, helping my classmates improve their resumes, and practicing mock interviews so they could land internships and post-graduate jobs. I even made weekly stops at the local plasma and blood donation centers to earn money donating plasma from my body (one hour paid $100). All this to afford rent, feed my wife and me, keep the lights on, pay for gasoline, and to maintain my seat at the mastermind table.

As one of the hardest working members in my first mastermind, I competed for the first Opportunity Chair (a position that allowed mastermind members to be featured for a select timeframe and earn counsel from the other members) each week, which meant that I could report on my progress towards my goals and be the first to share my newest challenges. I worked so hard so that people knew that I was qualified and meant to be in that board room. I was jobless but the most valuable player in the room. Within just a few months, I had a job as an accountability coach, owned several businesses and side hustles, and nearly doubled my salary at my previous job, all through the merits of my hard work and application from the mastermind group. It was the perfect environment to accelerate my results and help me achieve my goals.

Although I worked hard, 12 other people in my mastermind still competed for a time in the Opportunity Chair, as they called it. Equally to receiving counsel and feedback from this mastermind was my desire to give as many resources as possible and connections to the other members. I knew the more I poured into this mastermind, the more I would take away from it. It was my goal to make sure I paid particular attention to each member's needs and would do my research to help find ways to help them. Each member has their own unique success story. Here are a few:

> **Concierge Suit Tailor:** A suit tailor who developed a local subscription-based business model where he initially visits a client's home to get customer measurements. Then he imports materials and crafts together custom-cut suits each month for his clients. Within this mastermind, his social media presence grew by thousands, and his customer pool tripled within three months.

Synthetic Hair Extension Retailer: A side hustle started on Etsy.com, making synthetic dreadlocks quickly turned into an international trend as the Dreadful Hippie. Thousands of people worldwide are ordering and wearing their Synthetic, washable, clean, and easily installable dreadlocks. It became a global fashion statement for men and women who wanted to feel more confident in themselves. That global virality spark derived from the mastermind's counsel and accountability.

Sales Director for a Startup: A small startup sales company selling daily fantasy sports statistical picks and weekly winner-board prizes quickly grew from 10 to over 300 salespersons and a half-million dollar annual earning within its first six months. In case you were wondering, we watched the director go from driving a pick-up truck to his dream car, a Porsche 911, in only a few months. The mastermind's vast wealth of connections and referrals inspired massive growth in the company.

Health Coach: A health coach who went from 280 pounds to 190 pounds and a six-pack in six months found ways to tell his story better and earned himself more clients faster than he could keep up. The biggest takeaway from their business was that they didn't need to go beg for clients. Instead, he was able to turn away prospects and work with exactly his ideal clients.

Real Estate Photographer: An 18-year-old newly graduated youngster decided his nice camera and the new drone would make an excellent pair for doing fly-over real estate footage for local realtors and brokers. This move changed his life as he went from quitting his day job at an ice cream parlor to making over six figures by selling his services and photography.

These were only a select few achievers in this mastermind group. The mastermind journey was transformational for all of those involved. In each meeting, we wanted to help each other succeed and witnessed incredible growth within just a few months. Thus, the power of the mastermind methods was in motion.

The Anatomy of a Mastermind

In Napoleon Hill's *Think and Grow Rich,* he describes the mastermind as an "organized effort produced through the coordination of effort of two or more people, who work toward a definite end, in a spirit of harmony." In modern English, two or more people gather in agreement or consent to reach a desired outcome. Hill says, "plans are inert and useless, without sufficient power to translate them into action." The power, Hill describes, has the components of infinite intelligence, accumulated experience, and experiment and research results. Knowledge can be acquired through any of those sources and can be converted into power by organizing them into plans of action.

I observed that this professionally organized and facilitated mastermind I had the privilege of attending had several key components that made up the foundations for a successful mastermind group with two or more people. They include:

1. *A leader and facilitator* who organized and scheduled the meeting of all its members.
2. *A room and environment* where harmony could reside and trust could be given.
3. *A scribe* who took the minutes and respectfully held each member accountable for their commitments and declarations.
4. *A set of rules and expectations* for membership behavior and how the room would be conducted.
5. *An agreement* signed by each member, which protected the intellectual property and the business ideas shared amongst the group.
6. *A democratic list of consequences* for failure to take action toward a member's commitments and declarations.

7. **A *timekeeper*** who helped the group stay time-aware and efficient to the boundaries set within each meeting.
8. **A *focused group*** with zero distractions.
9. **A *common belief*** and mindset that the more each person shares counsel, ideas, resources, guidance, and connections that they will reap the benefits of serving their fellow men and women.
10. **A *public commitment*** and declaration by each attending member as to which actions they plan to take in the time between the next meeting.

All these components operated in unison and agreement, which became our Ten Commandments of Mastermind Membership. Not all masterminds and groups have, nor needed, a strict agreement as suggested above. The agreements, environment, leadership, structure, and acceptance of each person is absolutely vital to the progress which ignites the power the mastermind influenced in each of our lives and businesses.

My Desire to Learn More

Fascinated by this process and how it truly makes a difference in the lives of those who pursue it, I began inquiring more about running mastermind groups. On occasion, the group facilitator would ask me to run the group while he took notes. That evolved into filling in for them when they were sick or had personal emergencies. Which ultimately turned my apprenticeship into a full-time responsibility. I loved arriving early, preparing the boardroom, turning the environment into a success haven, and reviewing the accountability reports and follow-up proceedings. I treated this new opportunity as if I were running the first congressional conference in 1789, where the US Constitution formed. Within the first year of taking over and running these meetings, I put in about 1,000 hours of running, facilitating, and training in these small group masterminds.

Latinos In Action

My colleagues who invited me into this magical method had been training other companies how to implement mastermind methods within their organizations. I got a call to attend a local leadership training event for the organization formally known as LIA (Latinos In Action). There, I spent several hours with young professionals as we taught, practiced, and facilitated group masterminds to these aspiring leaders. It was a hit! Soon I was flying to Florida and training at the national leadership conference. This led to speaking opportunities at the university level and even to the C-Suite.

In one training, we had a young girl share her personal story of going to school and learning as best she could, so she could change her family's legacy. They were poor, alcoholics, and drug- driven. She wanted so badly to get scholarships and a top-tier education to provide for her family. This remarkable dream quickly turned the classroom into a frenzy for ideas, resources, counsel, and support. The girl, who will change her family forever, was in tears at the support of the mastermind group and the clarity she received as a result of her openness and gratitude for all the ideas she shared. The young women's example was one of hundreds of stories and examples that blossomed from that training and to the members of that respected organization. I learned that these principles help business owners in the boardroom and young aspiring leaders, youth, and dreamers.

Amplified Minds

The startup company that allowed me these traveling, training, and speaking opportunities regarding the mastermind group and principles was an organization called Amplified Minds, founded by Matthew Fritzsche and Brian Hubbard. They initially brought me on board to grow their marketing and public relations. We soon transitioned into having me perform the accountability coaching, facilitating the various mastermind groups, and running the podcast and events. After one year of working for this company, I was promoted to the President position for my leadership and dedication to the growth of our mission, where we focused our efforts on accountability coaching and follow-up through masterminds. This position allowed me more opportunities to travel the country, visit and study other mastermind events, and learn what it would take to become a global mastermind leader.

Prosperity Gym & PROFIT Mastermind

Locally in Utah, a small mastermind group complimented some of our Amplified Minds groups called Prosperity Gym. We met at a private shooting range and gun club lounge to meet monthly. The founder and creator were Levi McPherson, who created an acronym to help us practice our monthly mastermind sessions and growth. The abbreviation was PROFIT, which stood for People, Resources, Opportunities, Funding, Information, and Technology. If you'd like a more in-depth dive into this method, turn to the chapter in this book by Gina Bacalski. Like the last mastermind group I joined, I quickly became a teaching asset in this group and started running and leading local groups. I guess I had a knack for throwing myself 100% in with these mastermind groups.

We merged the Amplified Minds methods and the Prosperity Gym network and formed a local free mastermind group at the Ignite Recording Studios in downtown Salt Lake City. We called it the PROFIT Mastermind, where we focused on leading activities that would build trust quickly and lead to forming connections that created increased profits for everyone. It was free because we were testing a theory: How much money could be transacted between members by adding fun, recreational activities, and trust-building sequences before performing the mastermind methods of PROFIT channel identifiers.

The results were outstanding as we followed up and collected data from each participant over nine months. Within that timeframe, over $20 million had been transacted between members due to the shared counsel.

This was a lowball estimate based on the reports and numbers gathered during and after each event. When we realized we were sitting on a gold mine of $20 million worth of profits and productivity, we knew it was time to build an environment for champions. Thus, Champion Circle was born.

Champion Circle

We had proven to ourselves that networking + fun + masterminds = $20 million or more in a short period. It was time to build a company and model that would give this money multiplier a chance for other people to reap its benefits. Thus birthed the Champion Circle Networking Association— a networking group that focuses on the recreational discoveries of Amplified Minds and the mastermind methods discovered in Napoleon Hill's *Think and Grow Rich*.

From quitting my corporate dream job to the creation of Champion Circle, many hours had been dedicated to the participation, learning, leading, facilitating, organizing, coaching, mentoring, and launching masterminds both in-person and virtually through skype, zoom, Webex, Facetime, Google meet, WhatsApp, and even Facebook Messenger video calls. I've calculated several thousand hours of mastermind experience. But the experience isn't about becoming something; it's more importantly about the people this line of service can serve and help. Leading masterminds has become a mortal mission to serve humanity in escaping the monotony and finding accelerated results, which is why I've taken every opportunity to help build and lead great masterminds.

Habitude Warrior Mastermind & Global Speakers Mastermind

In 2020, speaker Erik "Mr. Awesome" Swanson approached me to help him grow and lead in the Habitude Warrior Mastermind. Created as a true organized mastermind in the Napoleon Hill way, Erik Swanson built the Habitude Warrior Mastermind to help mentor professionals through a virtual group forum and help them grow through their habits and attitudes. First, it was twice each month. Then we doubled in size and offered a second group, then a third. As the mastermind grew, we needed multiple platform forums to accommodate the flood of new members. A masterclass workshop was created to give members more networking and learning opportunities to grow their businesses called the Global Speakers Mastermind & Masterclass.

In the Global Speakers Mastermind, Erik Swanson invites his celebrity friends and connections to speak to our private mastermind community. Each session is uniquely different, alternating speaker keynotes with small mastermind meetings and counsel sessions. The groups are a massive success in helping members from all around the world, including the United States of America, Canada, United Kingdom, Mexico, Costa Rica, Australia, South Korea, Bali, and more.

Becoming A Global Mastermind Leader

Having now traveled and spoken about the mastermind methodologies to several countries, over 20 states, and so many different industries, I claim the title, but more importantly, the responsibility of Global Mastermind Leader. As an advocate, I feel a great deal of honor and perpetuate the sacred mastermind methodologies. The procedures in organized and unorganized masterminds have the divine principles of accessing infinite intelligence and harmony. It's no joke that the 'tenth step to riches' in Napoleon Hill's *Think and Grow Rich* is the conduit for prosperity and growth.

The world needs to experience true integrity-based masterminds through its result-creating methods. I believe masterminds can help anyone attain riches through the steps and qualities of clarity, desire, faith, auto-suggestion, specialized knowledge, imagination, planning, decision, persistence, transmutation, the subconscious mind, the brain, and one's sixth sense.

My vision and mission is to teach mastermind methods to as many people as possible. I believe the mastermind method can be used for good. It should be a standard practice in every family, school, college, church, boardroom, corporation, municipality, and government organization. That integrity can and will make the world a better place for all.

Many of my stories, notes, journals, discoveries, and experiences have been detailed in my book, *The Mastermind Manifesto,* releasing in 2023. In the manifesto, I share mastermind methodologies to accelerate results for each entity and give you a clear vision of which mastermind you should join to obtain the greatest results. If you are seeking to grow your habits, attitudes, and business on *Think and Grow Rich* principles, I highly recommend and invite you to join us in the Habitude Warrior Mastermind. Each week, our members are achieving their goals, getting insightful support and counsel, and achieving the results they desire. So join this tribe and become a Habitude Warrior for personal success! Grab a free pass to check us out at www.RideAlongGuestPass.com.

JON KOVACH JR.

About Jon Kovach Jr.: Jon is an award-winning and international motivational speaker and global mastermind leader. Jon has helped multi-billion-dollar corporations, including Coldwell Banker Commercial, Outdoor Retailer Cotopaxi, and the Public Relations Student Society of America, exceed their annual sales goals. In his work as an accountability coach and mastermind facilitator, Jon has helped thousands of professionals overcome their challenges and achieve their goals by implementing his accountability strategies and Irrefutable Laws of High Performance.

Jon is the Founder and Chairman of Champion Circle, a networking association that combines high-performance-based networking activities and recreational fun to create connection capital and increase prosperity for professionals.

Jon is the Mastermind Facilitator and Team Lead of the Habitude Warrior Mastermind and the Global Speakers Mastermind & Masterclass founded by Speaker Erik "Mr. Awesome" Swanson.

Jon speaks on a number of topics, including accountability, The Irrefutable Laws of High Performance, and The Power of Mastermind Methodologies. He is a #1 Best-Selling Author and was recently featured on SpeakUp TV, an Amazon Prime TV series, with his keynote speech titled, Getting Unstuck. He stars in over 100 speaking stages, podcasts, and live international summits on an annual basis.

Author's website: *www.JonKovachJr.com*
Book Series Website & Author's Bio: *www.The13StepsToRiches.com*

Amado Hernandez

CONTROL YOUR MIND

There were thirteen men in Leonardo da Vinci's famous mural of *The Last Supper*. Most of the men were fishermen turned holy men. One was a nobleman, and one was a tax collector. One would eventually betray all the others. They were history's most famous mastermind alliance.

Napoleon Hill is credited with introducing the concept of the "mastermind alliance." Yet, Andrew Carnegie recognized the significance of Jesus Christ and his Twelve Disciples as a mastermind group and shared that observation with Hill.

There are more interpretations of the mastermind alliance than there are flavors of Ben & Jerry's ice cream. And they range in size, diversity, and purpose from two Neanderthals huddling in a cave to our modern-day United Nations with 193 member states.

Franklin D. Roosevelt had his Brain Trust, and John F. Kennedy engaged the best and the brightest economic, political, and military advisors. Churchill had his war ministry. And Hitler had his Reich Cabinet of National Salvation.

In business, from the smallest to the largest corporation, there are members of the board of directors and advisors brainstorming and guiding the company's future. A New York Post article dated May 5, 2022, is titled "Meet Elon Musk's Inner Circle" and reports: "…the world's richest man continues to consult with a coterie of loyal confidants, investors, board members and researchers who are part of his inner circle."

Two hundred years before Napoleon Hill popularized the concept of the mastermind alliance, Benjamin Franklin formed his own mastermind group. In the fall of 1727, Franklin and his friends founded the Junto Club. Also known as the Leather Apron Club, the members met for 38 years on Friday evenings to discuss morals, politics, and natural philosophy. Franklin's Leather Apron Club undoubtedly contributed to his many inventions and accomplishments, even though he is depicted alone flying his kite in the rain to attract electricity.

There are open masterminds with no cost and elite masterminds costing tens of thousands of dollars a year. You can start one or join one. They can be up and personal or virtual. The caveat is that, like Newton's Third Law (for every action, there is an equal and opposite reaction), when there are "two or more minds working actively together in perfect harmony toward a common definite object" (Napoleon Hill – Laws of Success) that "common definite objective" can be either a positive or negative objective.

Our lives are full of mastermind alliances: past, present, and future. Sadly, the mastermind alliances that have pursued or achieved negative objectives most often come to mind before the positive ones. We may be more likely to conjure up visions of Adolph Hitler in a war room surrounded by generals and admirals planning to take over the world before we think about King Arthur and his Knights of the Round Table. William Shakespeare summed it up when he wrote: "The evil that men do lives after them; the good is oft interred with their bones." Mastermind alliances are perceived as large and small; transparent and conspiratorial; good and bad; famous and infamous.

There is also the perception of a "mastermind" referring to our own mind: the mind that God loaned to us during our individual lifetimes to achieve more than merely controlling our own bodies but to control our own destinies.

Think about these characteristics of our minds that you may or may not know. Our mind contains billions of brain cells, and information travels to and from our brain at 250 miles per hour, faster than a Formula One race car. Our mind cannot concentrate on more than one thing at a time, nor can it learn more than one thing at a time. And switching back and forth between tasks decreases productivity and results in declining mental performance and a shortened attention span.

So what does all that mean to us? Like life itself, our minds are God's greatest gifts. Not only do they allow us to dream, they enable us to pursue our dreams. The operative word is pursue. Our mind can become our best friend or our best enemy. So, what do we do about that? Here's the secret sauce: when you think about mastermind, think about your motivation and dedication to master your own mind. Become a mastermind. Reimagine the way you want to live your life and make your own dreams come true.

Easier said than done? Not really. Easier done than said. In *Think and Grow Rich* (1937), Napoleon Hill told us: "Whatever your mind can conceive and believe, it can achieve." And that's the real meaning of a mastermind. Picture a mastermind being an eight-cylinder engine. When all cylinders are firing properly, the engine is smooth and powerful. However, when one or more cylinders are not functioning as they should, the engine loses power or may even stop running.

So how do we get our minds to consistently run on all cylinders? A great way to begin is with gratitude, to continually thank God for the opportunity to live and positively impact our own lives and the lives of others. Keep in mind *Luke 12:48*: "To whom much is given, much will be required." You have been blessed with the priceless gifts of life, talent, knowledge, and time. Discover your own opportunities. Don't be afraid to fall and get scratched up once and a while. Pick yourself up and allow yourself time to heal. Then, rip off the bandage and head on out again without fear. Although pain is processed by our mind, the organ itself feels no pain.

Our mind is the world's smallest, fastest, and most powerful megacomputer. And has the ability to transmit and receive information to other minds in nanoseconds (faster than electronically processing your credit or debit card). So think about how you are sending and receiving thoughts and energy to others.

Be conscious of the effect you have on others. That effect originates in your mind. Try to be like Charlie Brown as described by Rod McKuen (A Boy Named Charlie Brown — 1969):

> *Like the shadows of the morning,*
> *Climb up to the August afternoon,*
> *Charlie has a way*
> *Of picking up the day,*
> *Just by walking slowly in a room.*
> *Maybe it's a kind of magic,*
> *That only little boys can do,*
> *But seeing Charlie smile,*
> *Can make you stop a while*
> *And get you feeling glad you're you.*
> *He's only a boy named Charlie,*
> *a boy named Charlie Brown.*
> *He's just a kid next door,*
> *perhaps a little more.*
> *He's every kid in every town.*
> *The world is full of lots of people,*
> *here and there and all around.*
> *But people, after all, Start out as being small,*
> *and we're all a boy named…*
> *~ Charlie Brown*

So maybe you don't need a mastermind alliance to be wealthy, healthy, and happy, or maybe you do. For some people, having others involved in their dreams and projects is critical to their success. Some need the support, accountability, and guidance of others; they need to belong and be a part of something. Others don't; they are self-motivated and self-managed. And it's not always one or the other. It all depends on who you are, who you want to be, and your level of confidence and independence.

Think of your mind as a kaleidoscope. Remember that little toy you would hold up to the light while twisting the end to change the colorful images? Likewise, your mind is a virtual kaleidoscope. There are no two images, no two experiences, exactly alike.

MasterMind or Master Mind? It really doesn't matter. Take control of your own mind. Feed it., nurture it, exercise it, and grow it. Push it to the limit. Continually rewire it and reprogram it, just like twisting the end of your kaleidoscope. Use your mind wisely to create extraordinary memories and leave your mark on your community and society.

Take nothing for granted. Remember that God made you a mastermind. Be humble. Be grateful. Always be generous and help others. Understand your ego as it relates to your mind. Your ego is part of your conscious personality and has the potential to sabotage your entire being. It's your self-awareness and what you try to project to others. In the final analysis, it is the mediator between an unrealistic or distorted internal idea (source of psychic energy) and a "realistic" outside world.

The best of both worlds, if you believe that you have control of your own mind, is to start and manage your own mastermind group. The greatest compliment to your mind is freely sharing your knowledge, talent, and passion with others. Think of Charlie Brown the next time you walk into a room. Spread your own kind of love and magic—from your own mastermind.

Dare to be great. Reimagine the way you live your life. Reach for the stars—the farthest ones. Hold on tight to your dreams—all of them. Dance on the edge. Color outside the lines and erase and redraw some of them once in a while just for fun. Expect the extraordinary. You are a MASTERMIND.

AMADO HERNANDEZ

About Amado Hernandez: Amado was born in Mexico of humble beginnings and raised in Los Angeles, California. As an avid reader, Amado always focused on self-development. He coaches sales professionals to make six and seven figures in real estate.

Amado believes in a progressive culture, one people-centric where clients' dreams come true and salespeople thrive; at the end of the day, we all want to be respected and pursue our happiness. My goal is to leave a legacy- making a difference in people's lives.

With 33 years of Real Estate experience, Mr. ABC Amado Hernandez successfully operates and grows his Excellence Empire Real Estate Moreno Valley office. Broker/Owner Amado first opened his doors in 1995, and Excellence currently has over 60 offices in Southern California, Las Vegas, Merida Yucatan, Mexico, and over 1,000 Agents. He is also part owner of a highly successful Mortgage company Excellence Mortgage and owner of Empire Escrow Services. Mr. Amado is also involved with his community and currently serves as Director at Inland Valley Association of Realtors and will be the President-Elect for 2023. Amado serves as a Director of CAR (California Association of Realtors).

Author's Website: *www.ExcellenceEmpireRE.com*
Book Series Website & Author's Bio: *www.The13StepsToRiches.com*

Angelika Ullsperger

SHARING INFINITE KNOWLEDGE

The power of belonging to a Mastermind group cannot be overstated.

Having a group of individuals who come together to support and challenge each other to achieve their goals can propel you forwards in your success. These groups can be a powerful resource for personal and professional growth, networking, idea generation, and more. The main point is Masterminds are of infinite value.

Everyone's story of joining a Mastermind is different. Some have the most life-changing realizations, while others are left with confusion, wondering what they need to do better. All Masterminds can provide knowledge, but not all Masterminds are equal. That is why joining the right one will prove invaluable to your efforts. For me, the most important aspect is a supportive and loving community that provides opportunities for professional and personal growth. Growth is an essential ingredient in creating a happy life, and Masterminds are a treasure trove if you're looking for growth.

At the beginning of my journey, I was incredibly lost. Not only was I lost, but the community I had surrounded myself with was not a healthy one. Living in and around Baltimore, I was constantly met with individuals who preferred drugs and crime. Growing up in a harsh environment, it's not fair to blame any of these people for their choices, but it was not what

I wanted for my life. Being surrounded by these individuals negatively impacted me, helping send me down a dark path in life. Chances are you've heard something like "Who you spend time with the most is who you will become" well, I knew with certainty this was not who I wanted to become. I realized if I'm to succeed, I need to change the network surrounding me. It was at the beginning of the covid pandemic when it hit me, yet this realization sent me on a journey at the best time. Because everyone was home, there was an exponential rise in online events.

I began to sign up for everything I could and considering it was all free, I went crazy. If I could sign up for it, I did. I repeated this over and over until the algorithms noticed and started recommending me events. At one of these events, Mel Mason's event, to be specific, I was invited on a ride-along for a Mastermind. A Mastermind? I had little idea what a Mastermind was at the time, but I've always been quick to jump at new opportunities, so I went. Little did I know the effects it would have. I found it right when I was starting to doubt if there were any truly good people out there. It was life changing. Never had I been part of a group so happy to help support others, and I loved it.

Being surrounded by a genuine, caring network of skilled and accomplished individuals has been a gift that has kept on giving. It's given me the opportunity to learn from their vast experiences and insights. You can only acquire so much life experience in a single lifetime when it's not humanly possible to go through every possible learning experience. Thankfully others have had those experiences and are willing to share what they have learned. For life-long growth, it becomes pertinent to stay open-minded and learn from the life experiences of others. I've been able to avoid certain mistakes due to the wisdom other members have shared with me, allowing me to save time and money.

In addition to the knowledge and expertise of the other group members, participating in a Mastermind group has also helped me develop my skills and capabilities. It can be hard to see the bigger picture when you're up close, but when you have a trustworthy community, others can point out skills you need or areas that could use improvement. Attending meetings has given me valuable experience in problem-solving and decision-making just by showing up with an open heart and open ears. I've grown exponentially by being exposed to new ideas and perspectives, many of which I have been able to apply to my own life and work.

Without others to share new ideas and perspectives, one may miss valuable learning opportunities and become narrow-minded and closed off to different viewpoints. This can lead to a lack of personal and professional growth and missed opportunities in all walks of life and collaborations. Without challenging our preconceived notions, we cannot broaden our understanding of the world. Luckily Mastermind groups are a great option to acquire a diverse source of information and engage with people with different experiences and expertise.

The accountability masterminds provide as well can make a massive difference. This key benefit has allowed me the opportunity to set and work toward specific, measurable goals. Sharing my goals with the group and receiving feedback and support has empowered me to stay focused and motivated, helping me to make significant progress in achieving my professional objectives.

Many of us have had loved ones who don't understand, won't support us, or worse, think we're crazy. I know when I told my mom I was writing a book and going to do a book signing, she thought I was losing it. Often these worries come from a place of love but end up discouraging. Therefore having a solid support system makes a massive difference in your likely hood of success. A good Mastermind group provides a safe and supportive environment for members to share their thoughts and feelings on various topics. This can broaden one's understanding of different approaches and techniques and stimulate creativity and innovation. By coming together regularly to share our goals, challenges, successes, and failures, others can offer advice, encouragement, and accountability, which helps to feel less alone in endeavors. It's easier to keep going when you see that others have successfully navigated similar terrain.

By sharing my goals with the group and receiving feedback and support, I have been able to stay focused and motivated, which has made significant progress in achieving my professional objectives. After joining a Mastermind, I accomplished many things in a relatively short time, such as becoming a #1 best-selling author several times, doing book signings, going to the world's #1 networking event, and a whole slew of additional accolades. Opportunities for learning and development are another critical benefit of Mastermind groups. Not only do members learn from each other, they learn from guest speakers and experts who help deepen one's knowledge and skills in a particular area and help identify areas for further learning and development.

Masterminds are the gift that keeps on giving. Another of these gifts has been building my professional network and reputation. This medium allowed me to meet more motivated individuals, leading me to become more motivated and work harder. As a by-product, I've met some of the world's most successful and inspiring people. But, more importantly, I've gotten to help and bring value to many. By participating in meetings and events regularly, I have made valuable connections and established myself as a thought leader and contributor in my field.

I am so blessed and infinitely grateful for these experiences. But, if we are being honest, I'm not sure I would have experienced any of those magical moments if I hadn't decided to join a Mastermind. Not only have I grown significantly in my career, but I've also grown immensely in my personal life. Everything accumulatively allowed me to be better and show up for the people I love. It's given me a greater reach to make a positive impact. With these gifts, I've been able to create more happiness and success in my own life, allowing me to bring these gifts to others.

ANGELIKA ULLSPERGER

About Angelika Ullsperger: Angelika is a serial entrepreneur from Baltimore, Maryland. She is a fashion designer, model, artist, photographer, and musician. Angelika has extensive and well-rounded professional experience having worked as a business owner, carpenter, chef, graphic designer, manager, event planner, sales and product specialist, marketer, and coach. Angelika is now a #1 Best-Selling Author in the historic book series, *The 13 Steps To Riches*. She is a life-long learner with a sincere and genuine interest in all things of the world with a major interest in the formal subject of abnormal psychology, neuroscience, and quantum physics.

Angelika prides herself as someone who has saved lives as a friend, first responder, EMT, and knowledgeable suicide prevention advocate. With a vast knowledge and experience in multiple professions, Angelika is also a proud honorable member of Phi Theta Kappa, The APA, the AAAS, and an FBLA (Future Business Leaders Association) Business Competition Finalist. She is Certified in basic coding and blockchain technology. Amongst the careers and vast experience, Angelika is an adventurer and avid dog lover.

Her ultimate goals and dreams are to make a lasting positive impact in people's lives through her wealth of knowledge and skillsets.

Author's Website: *www.Angelika.world*

Book Series Website & Author's Bio: *www.The13StepsToRiches.com*

Dr. Anthony M. Criniti IV

WISELY COLLECT YOUR COLLECTIVE MIND

Think and Grow Rich by Napoleon Hill is one of the best classic books to teach someone about how to become a financial success (as well as a success in other areas of life). In there, you will find his thirteen steps to riches; each one has its own separate chapter and analysis. The subject of our book is to interpret his ninth step to riches: the power of the Master Mind. Let's review some of the major highlights of this chapter.

To help us to understand the subject of this extremely short chapter, Hill defined both of the key terms. First, he starts by providing a framework for explaining what power is. "Power is essential for success in the accumulation of money. Plans are inert and useless, without sufficient power to translate them into action. This chapter will describe how an individual may attain and apply power. Power may be defined as "organized and intelligently directed knowledge." Power, as the term is used here, refers to the organized effort sufficient to enable an individual to transmute desire into its monetary equivalent. An organized effort is produced through the coordination of effort of two or more people, who work toward a definite end, in a spirit of harmony" (Hill, 2011, p. 252).

Hill goes on to identify the three sources of knowledge: Infinite Intelligence, Accumulated Experience, and Experiment and Research (Hill, 2011, p. 252-253). Out of these three sources, Hill explains which one is the most significant: "The list of the chief sources from which power may be attained is, as you have seen, headed by infinite intelligence. When two or more people coordinate in a spirit of harmony and work toward a definite objective, they place themselves in a position, through that alliance, to absorb power directly from the great universal storehouse of Infinite Intelligence. This is the greatest of all sources of power. It is the source to which the genius turns. It is the source to which every great leader turns (whether he may be conscious of the fact or not). The other two major sources from which the knowledge necessary for the accumulation of power may be obtained are no more reliable than the five senses of man. The senses are not always reliable. Infinite Intelligence does not err" (Hill, 2011, p. 258-259).

Hill also defines and explains the concept of the Master Mind: "The "Master Mind" may be defined as coordination of knowledge and effort, in a spirit of harmony, between two or more people, for the attainment of a definite purpose. No individual may have great power without availing himself of the "Master Mind." In a preceding chapter, instructions were given for the creation of plans for the purpose of translating desire into its monetary equivalent. If you carry out these instructions with persistence and intelligence and use discrimination in the selection of your "Master Mind" group, your objective will have been halfway reached, even before you begin to recognize it" (Hill, 2011, p. 253-254).

The Master Mind is an extremely important concept that is a foundation for the science of success. The idea behind this is that the whole is greater than the sum of its parts. The more great minds come together, the stronger the collective unit becomes. Hill calls this the "third mind:" "No two minds ever come together without, thereby, creating a third, invisible, intangible force which may be likened to a third mind" (Hill, 2011, p. 254).

Hill is no stranger to the concept of the Master Mind. Actually, it is a part of the reason that he became successful. That is, he surrounded himself with some of the most successful people of his day. These people also had Master-Minded with other extremely successful people. Excuse the pun; as you will read next, steel sharpened steel.

Hill explains: "The Master Mind principle, or rather the economic feature of it, was first called to my attention by Andrew Carnegie over twenty-five years ago. The Discovery of this principle was responsible for the choice of my life's work. Mr. Carnegie's Master Mind group consisted of a staff of approximately fifty men, with whom he surrounded himself, for the definite purpose of manufacturing and marketing steel. He attributed his entire fortune to the power he accumulated through this "Master Mind." Analyze the record of any man who has accumulated a great fortune and many of those who have accumulated modest fortunes. You will find that they have either consciously or unconsciously employed the "Master Mind" principle" (Hill, 2011, p. 255).

The concept of the Master Mind is important in good and bad economic times. Hill knows that very well, as he wrote *Think and Grow Rich* during the Great Depression. Hill describes the process of alternating between being rich and poor: "Some people undergo the experience of alternating between the positive and negative sides of the stream, being at times on the positive side, and at times on the negative side. The Wall Street crash of '29 swept millions of people from the positive to the negative side of the stream. These millions are struggling, some of them in desperation and fear, to get back to the positive side of the stream. This book was written especially for those millions. Poverty and riches often change places. The Crash taught the world this truth, although the world will not long remember the lesson. Poverty may, and generally does, voluntarily take the place of riches. When riches take the place of poverty, the change is usually brought about through well-conceived and carefully executed PLANS. Poverty needs no plan. It needs no one to aid it, because it is bold and ruthless. Riches are shy and timid. They have to be "attracted" (Hill, 2011, p. 260-261).

Indeed, there are countless examples of when poverty takes the place of riches. We can take our clues from all over history. Two moments full of examples include The Great Depression and the end of the Roman era. As stated in Principle 68 of *The Most Important Lessons in Economics and Finance:* "There is no such thing as a permanent Caesar" (Criniti, 2014, p. 100).

The process that Hill described during the Wall Street Crash is interrelated to a process called The Survival-Prosperity Sequence discussed in my third book called the Survival of the Richest. In an individual's lifetime, he or she could move back and forth between survival and prosperity steps depending on the fluctuation of his or her wealth. Everything is at stake if wealth is not managed properly. As stated in The Necessity of Finance: "Thus the management of wealth in order to meet the goal of continuously maximizing wealth becomes a condition for individual survival" (Criniti, 2013, p. 47).

When wealth is minimized, you could be pulled closer to what I call the Edge of Survival. *From The Survival of the Richest*: "The essence of prosperity is to stay as far away from the edge of survival as you can, for this is one place where second chances rarely exist. If you fall over its edge, then death might be inevitable" (Criniti, 2016, p. 160). In regard to poverty, as Hill referenced previously, this is a very dangerous place. "Living in absolute poverty is living below the edge of survival, which may be only a short distance from death" (Criniti, 2016, p. 165).

To conclude, applying the Master Mind is critical to being highly successful. This concept works for everyone in all industries. As for the ideal number of people in a Master Mind, the answer varies. Motivational speaker Jim Rohn was known to have said that we are the average of the 5 people that we spend the most time with. As was noted in the quote from Hill above, Andrew Carnegie's magic number was probably about 50. Also, the Master Mind has always been working, even before it got its name. For example, Jesus had a Master Mind with roughly 12 others (called the 12 Apostles) about 2,000 years ago.

Whether it is 5, 12, or 50, the strength of the Master Mind is not found as much in the strength of its numbers as it is in the strength of its Collective Mind. Hill mentioned the "third mind" as an example when there are two people in the group. However, if there were 50 people in the group, then his title would change to the "fifty-first mind." The main idea is that the Collective Mind is more powerful than the sum of the minds of each of the individual members alone. All of the minds united can become an unstoppable force when thinking as one. This point highlights the significance of being highly selective of whom you trust to be in this life-changing group. A Master Mind of a small group of insecure, miserable people can lead to an insecure, miserable existence. The opposite is also true.

In short, it's not the exact number of people in a Master Mind but the quality of its members that dictates success. To master your mind, you must choose wisely your Master Mind.

Bibliography

Criniti, Anthony M., IV. 2013. The Necessity of Finance: An Overview of the Science of Management of Wealth for an Individual, a Group, or an Organization. Philadelphia: Criniti Publishing.

Criniti, Anthony M., IV. 2014. The Most Important Lessons in Economics and Finance: A Comprehensive Collection of Time-Tested Principles of Wealth Management. Philadelphia: Criniti Publishing.

Criniti, Anthony M., IV. 2016. The Survival of the Richest: An Analysis of the Relationship between the Sciences of Biology, Economics, Finance, and Survivalism. Philadelphia: Criniti Publishing.

Hill, Napoleon. 2011. *Think and Grow Rich*. United Kingdom: Capstone Publishing Ltd.

DR. ANTHONY M. CRINITI

About Dr. Anthony M. Criniti IV: Dr. Anthony M. Criniti IV (aka "Dr. Finance®") is the world's leading financial scientist and survivalist. A fifth generation native of Philadelphia, Dr. Criniti is a former finance professor at several universities, a former financial planner, an active investor in diverse marketplaces, an explorer, an international keynote speaker, and has traveled around the world studying various aspects of finance. He is an award winning author of three #1 international best-selling finance books: The Necessity of Finance (2013), The Most Important Lessons in Economics and Finance (2014), and The Survival of the Richest (2016). Dr. Criniti is also the host of the highly successful Dr. Finance® Live Podcast as well as one of the top hosts on Clubhouse. Dr. Criniti has started a grassroots movement that is changing the way that we think about economics and finance. Learn more about Doctor Finance at DrFinance.Info.

Author's website: *www.DrFinance.info*
Book Series Website & Author's Bio: *www.The13StepsToRiches.com*

Barry Bevier

THE POWER OF THE MASTERMIND — THE HOT SEAT

I've been truly blessed to be in the well-organized Yes - Mastermind for several years. When people don't know about the Mastermind concept and ask me what it is, my short response is "Organized Brainstorming on Steroids." Napoleon Hill considered the Mastermind one of the most important principles in his book. In his words, he describes the Mastermind as "consisting of two or more people who work in perfect harmony for the attainment of a definite purpose."

It is the principle through which you may borrow and use the education, experience, influence, and perhaps the capital of other people in carrying out your own plans in life. It is the principle through which you can accomplish in one year more than you could accomplish without it in a lifetime if you depended entirely upon your own efforts for success. Being a spiritual person, Napoleon Hill describes that perhaps the first known Mastermind existed between Jesus and his 12 Disciples. He also points out that the Declaration of Independence is one of the best examples of the Mastermind principle. Fifty-six men banded together with the intent to change the direction of history in America. They composed and signed the Declaration of Independence, knowing full well that it might turn out to either be freedom for all mankind or a death warrant where each of the signers could be hanged. Although not formal, most of us have likely been involved in some sort of Mastermind throughout our lives. In school or college, we may have participated in study groups. Book Clubs & Bible Studies may be considered a form of a Mastermind where the participants share ideas and have the opportunity to gain a better knowledge of what they are discussing.

Book four of our *13 Steps to Riches* series focused on the principle of Specialized Knowledge and its importance in gaining success. The Mastermind is a perfect way to obtain and leverage specialized knowledge from others. Many of the successful industrialists that Napoleon Hill interviewed over the course of more than 20 years had little education or knowledge in the field where they were extremely successful. This was because they had a Mastermind with people with the knowledge needed for their business success.

Hill says power is essential for success in the accumulation of money. Often, plans are inert and useless without sufficient power to translate them into action. I think one of the challenges we have as entrepreneurs is that we feel we have to create a plan, complete with all the details. We attempt to mitigate risk and liability. We are seeking the fastest path to profit and success. We are seeking the biggest impact that we can have. We think that we must have a detailed plan before we can get started putting it into action. We have to know how we're going to do everything. Hill says plans are useless. Plans are derived at our level of awareness, based on the conditions and circumstances that exist at the time and what we are aware of. Often, those conditions and circumstances change, and our awareness may also change.

When we are in a Mastermind, we bring our ideas to others who give us their input. Ideas that will expand our awareness and will deepen our understanding of the conditions and circumstances. There will be different perspectives that perhaps we didn't think of before. Our awareness absolutely can change when we are in a Mastermind. Working out our plan with the assistance of a Mastermind will almost always result in a much better plan with the accountability to get started, even before the plan is complete. One of my Mentors, Paul Martinelli, says, "Jump and build your wings and on the way make the plan as you go," and Martin Luther King is quoted as saying, "You don't need to see the whole staircase to take the first step."

The power of the Mastermind is forged by an environment where collective knowledge and experience are leveraged. The Yes - Mastermind of which I'm a member is led by Patrick Carney, who, amazingly, has held Mastermind groups for over 40 years. Patrick is extremely well-versed in optimizing the effectiveness and efficiency of the Mastermind principles. There are typically 12 members, and our weekly meetings are structured and disciplined. A high level of attendance is required, and every member is expected to play full out at every meeting. Attendance is important. When attendance is not required, the Know, Like, and Trust factor for members to be open and transparent does not exist. During each gathering, each member has five minutes to share what's going on in their life. Specifically, we are asked to have a Gratitude, a Success, a Challenge, a Stretch Goal for the week, and an Ask. The Ask is very important. Many people are reluctant to ask for assistance or guidance. The Mastermind provides a safe environment for any member to ask for something that they need to help them move forward during the next week.

Twice a month, one member has the opportunity to have a Hot Seat. The Hot Seat is where the magic comes into the Mastermind concept. The member on the Hot Seat has 15 minutes to present a topic they are looking for assistance with from the 11 other Mastermind members. During this 15-minute period, the other members must remain silent and not interrupt the presentation. This is very important, as it gives the member on the Hot Seat the opportunity to remain focused on the presentation or their ideas.

The presentation is followed by a few minutes for clarifying questions, and then the magic starts. The member on the Hot Seat must remain silent and as expressionless as possible while the other members, one at a time, provide their input, also without interrupting each other or being negative about another's ideas. A safe environment of open thinking is important to encourage the flow of creativity. This is where the "third mind in the ether" that Napoleon Hill refers to comes into play. Several people may offer their comments and suggestions. New ideas are triggered by those thoughts, and the process continues for an hour. During the time I've been in the Mastermind, I have observed several people develop clarity and direction, including me. Great ideas for new businesses or reviving and expanding an existing business or project have been conceived and brought to reality through the Hot Seat process. I have also found that I get almost as much from the other members' Hot Seats as I do from my own. Throughout the lifespan of Patrick's Mastermind, over 50 books have been created or advanced through the Hot Seat process and ultimately published.

In writing this chapter, I asked the members of my Mastermind to provide their biggest takeaways from being in the Mastermind. Here are a few of the comments:

    Expands our own ideas and produces help for areas needed
    Moves ideas and new concepts into reality
    Creates a cross-pollination of ideas Inspires new ideas
    Motivates us to take more action sooner
    Learning from high-level guest speakers and trainers
    Meaningful and lasting relationships, comradery
    Motivation to give back or reciprocate and help other members
    Creates deeper introspection and self-discovery
    Our Net Worth lies in our Network Builds confidence
    Accountability and encouragement to take action

I've been invited to participate in other "Masterminds" that have a very different, loosely structured format. "Masterminds" where the leader shares some of his experiences and then delivers a pitch for his next coaching program. I've been in "Masterminds" where the leader takes on the role of a coach or teacher, and the other members are not given the opportunity to express their ideas and opinions to the member on the "Hot Seat." I've been in "Masterminds" that have an open discussion where people interrupt each other, which can deflate the energy of the creative process.

Although some of our members get a little frustrated with the level of structure and discipline in the Mastermind that I'm in, those factors are essential in maintaining a productive environment that spurns new ideas and creativity.

I'm often asked if the 3-hour weekly time commitment to be in the Mastermind is worth it. My response is a resounding Yes, absolutely! Being in this Mastermind has provided me with insight, clarity, inspiration, and knowledge. It is helping me to take my business, relationships, and life to a new level. A level I would not otherwise have been able to achieve alone. Not only am I able to receive the help, encouragement, and accountability of 11 other brilliant minds, I can help others to get to new levels in their lives. To me, that is the most important part: giving back and paying it forward.

BARRY BEVIER

About Barry Bevier: Barry Bevier is a proud father of two amazing daughters in their mid-twenties, who are pursuing their passions in psychology and architecture in Southern California where he lived, worked and raised a family for over 40 years. He recently moved to North Carolina to pursue the next adventure in his life's journey. He was raised on a family farm near Ann Arbor, Michigan. Growing up, he developed his faith in God, a strong work ethic, a love for nature, and a passion to help others. After completing his master's degree in civil engineering at the University of Michigan, he pursued a career in engineering, which eventually brought him to Southern California.

In 2000, he married the love of his life, Linda. They shared a beautiful life for ten years, until she succumbed to the effects of lupus and 20 years of treatment with prescription medications. Since then, Barry pivoted his career path into educating and helping others. Barry has educated himself in alternative, natural modalities in wellness and became a Licensed Brain Health Expert through Amen Clinics. His primary focus and business is a new technology in stem cell supplementation that releases your own stem cells without invasive medical procedures.

Author's Website: *www.BRBevier.Stemtech.com*
Book Series Website & Author's Bio: *www.The13StepsToRiches.com*

Bonnie Lierse

POWERFUL MASTERMINDS ON STEROIDS

Can you be open to unusual ideas or something new and unexpected? Are you driven to evolve? Ask yourself, who am I?

I am living it!

Do you know the power of a mastermind? Have you ever been on one? We take for granted that everyone knows about them, but they truly do not! I know many individuals that have never experienced them! There is a difference in each of their personalities! Powerful!

When I look back on all my years of work and business ownership, masterminding was not the most popular subject. You never heard anyone talk about it. Of course, there were business meetings, but they were definitely not called "MASTERMINDS."

Now you have to ask yourself, how flexible am I to grow and change, especially with these times! Are you considered open-minded? There are "Summits" everywhere all over the world these days (even on Zoom and Facebook live), as well as masterminds from all different backgrounds and businesses. (Many free) We are in the millennium. Because of these outstanding masterminds, I've learned to read and listen to extraordinary mindsets. They certainly, developed and evolved me deeply.

Are you open to a new, unexpected path and journey, as I have been on? It's lighting me up! But, sometimes, it takes something deeply major to shake you, so you can say, "Ok, it's time!"

For me, it was losing my soulmate, best friend, hero, and husband back on November 23rd, 2021.

Is it your time to shine, move forward, stretch, and be the best you? It's all choice! Everything is a choice. Even the tears of grieving and how long you choose to do that. I am living it. You are in control of your destiny! No, it's not easy! Anything worthwhile is not easy. We are always being taught lessons on this earth. What are some of yours? My viewpoints have evolved. We will save that for a future read.

There are different types of masterminds. Some are specific toward a particular business, like mine in "Business Development and Leadership," and some like "Habitude Warriors." They help others on their own individual, personal journeys and specific paths. I have felt so freed because of this. I ask myself all the time, who am I, what do I desire, and what's my passion? It does start with a WHY. What's your WHY? Think about that. It's easy to forget what we really are destined for. I did as well. I am human! Living that journey and experience as we speak!

Because of Habitude Warriors, I am blessed and honored to stretch my journey into writing, one of my new WHYs. I am discovering who I am, just writing in this outstanding book series. It probably "wouldn't" have happened without this incredible mastermind. A door was meant to open (thank you, Erin Ley, who introduced me to this). It also brought me on my spiritual journey. (BABY-STEPS) I am learning to be organic and let things flow. That is something I've developed partly due to this mastermind mindset and partly to my medium readings and guidance. Learning to speak abundance, prosperity, and success is also a part of this, and surrendering things that won't serve you or me.

I am licensed in real estate in Virginia now (I was building real estate in New York before I moved to Virginia ten years ago). My goal is to find your dream home with less stress and much trust because it's one of the biggest purchases you make in a lifetime, or sell it with ease! We have many masterminds, even in real estate! They're powerful and can offer motivation, breathing, meditation, and gratitude!

Successful, like-minded businesspeople crave that success and that thought process. You'll always find them on a mastermind of some sort.

Masterminds teach me and others balance on so many levels! No individual is the same!

I have had many businesses over the years. There was always education regarding that business, but they weren't called masterminds then. Masterminds can be two individuals (I have many of those, where we brainstorm together) or maybe an infinite number of individuals.

It offers deep discussions about things you want to understand.

In a mastermind they help with belief in yourself! They help build you and remind you of your unique incredible gifts as they do for me. They can get you through emotional rollercoasters, as they are doing for me presently!

I was also blessed because I had a magical and deep mastermind with my husband, Tommy! He was well-versed in so many subjects. His brilliant mind encouraged and stretched me every day! Sometimes, we take things for granted. I'm still learning that lesson as we speak. I'm here to tell you, DON'T! It was a big hard lesson I had to learn after my husband's passing to the other side— plenty of sobbing! Really look at what you have around you!

Today, we can have masterminds in person or on zoom! What's even more sensational to me is that they can connect people from around the world!

These masterminds truly help me develop into the best me! I'm discovering who I am. Do you know who you are? I have a one-on-one with a medium from the UK. I was meant to meet him. Divine timing! He teaches me an incredible thought process most will never learn.

If you can get this from a mastermind, you have already won and are ahead of the game! On a great mastermind, they will build your confidence and courage and dig into who you truly are and what you are made of! This was written by my husband, Tommy Lierse, and I can tell you, he always built my confidence and belief in love and me.

Aspects of Love (Why the Love?)

Your DEVOTION to family is impressive.
Your EMPATHY cannot be more genuine.
Your RESPECT for me is heartening.
Your INTREPIDNESS is dauntless.
Your NURTURING is intense.
Your STRENGTH is bold.
Your CARING is sincere.
In short, your HEART is dearest of anyone I know.
To that special person in my life—It was to me.

Love, Tommy - March 18th, 2021
He wrote this just before he passed away!

He always reminded me of the things I forgot about myself! As I had with my Tommy, one-on- one masterminds will build you and yourself up. It will help develop and recognize your outstanding abilities. We never stop learning and growing; at least, I don't and won't! So ask yourself, will you?

On our masterminds, we share from the heart. I have learned to say what I am grateful for, do breathing techniques, meditate, and discovered journaling, which I love now!

You are so blessed to be in a world you can mastermind daily, weekly, or even monthly! Some of the masterminds, in the beginning, might play music or motivational YouTube inspirations, which definitely sends a positive energy flowing! We all need that positive energy and vibration!

Everyone is on a different journey, whether emotional, religious, spiritual, or something else! What is yours? Discover who you are at these masterminds or from an extraordinary husband, friend, family member like mine, or somewhere else! Someone that will build you up and recognize your qualities and gifts (like family). The beautiful part is: there are masterminds, not only for business but personal healing, developing yourself physically and mentally.

My daughter, Cassi, is developing a health coach business. Guaranteed, she is a part of many masterminds. My other daughter, Viktoria, does Reiki and more! Everything is about learning a particular field and developing that passion. My one son is in sales, and my other son is a firefighter. The focus should always be on your passion. I'm searching and developing that now. I am in love passionately with my spiritual journey or path. It has been a thousand-degree turnaround! My husband wrote this A-Z about the qualities he felt. If you can get this from a mastermind, you are ahead of the game! It should raise your belief and faith in yourself and life!

> My Dear Loves Attributes A-Z (my husband's perspective about me). Now that's a mastermind on steroids!
> Admirable
> Beautiful and Believing
> Caring
> Deep
> Ebullient
> Forgiving
> Giving and Grateful
> Honorable
> Inimitable

Joyful
Kind
Loving, lovable, and loyal
Merciful
Nurturing
Optimistic
Persistent and Punctual
Reliable
Spiritual
Talented and Tasteful
Understanding
Vivacious
Winsome
Exuberant
Young at heart
Zesty

Love, Tommy 12/2018

If someone will create that belief in you at a mastermind and remind you of your extraordinary qualities, you are ahead of most!

BONNIE LIERSE

About Bonnie Lierse: Bonnie Zaruches Lierse is extremely artistic and creative, with an entrepreneurial bent. Besides that, she is a seasoned agent with more than twenty years' experience in real estate in the New York/Long Island area. She relocated to Northern Virginia in 2012 and continued her real estate career there.

Another passion is creating leaders by working in business leadership development with *Leadership Team Development (LTD),* marketing products supplied by *Amway.* She was also a member of *The Screen Cartoonist Guild of Motion Pictures* for many years. Also, she did freelance for *Sesame Street* in New York City. In addition, she was a District Director for an interior accessory design company, as her own business.

Bonnie is blessed with five beautiful grandchildren and is very close with her children and family, some of whom are also in Virginia. Her missions, are leadership, mentorship, paying it forward, and changing lives one at a time. Her motto is "You be the difference!"

Author's Website: *www.amway.com/myshop/SplashFXEnterprises*
Book Series Website & Author's Bio: *www.The13StepsToRiches.com*

Brian Schulman

TOGETHER WE DO

"A group of people who complement each other in order to accomplish a goal." This is what Napoleon Hill defined as a Mastermind. Different knowledge across the board, yes, but the same mindset, each showing a positive attitude toward helping the other.

Masterminds are ideal because they bring together people with a wide range of skills and knowledge that contribute to accomplishing the goal.

Two requirements must be met when creating a mastermind to achieve its purpose. First, members must have a solid understanding of one another. To mesh as a true team, the connection must satisfy, be useful, and be valuable to each member on an intellectual and emotional level.

There is an element of a mastermind in every successful business venture. Companies with a well- organized group of experts at the top complement one another's areas of expertise and regularly collaborate with the same goal of creating and maintaining a successful business.

Masterminds can be any size, from five people or 50+ people. The right number depends on your goal, the skills needed to accomplish that goal, and the ability of the whole to communicate and work effectively together. Masterminds can be for any purpose. The key is having a clearly defined end goal.

COVID impacted everyone, everywhere. Overnight, you knew someone who was sick, died, lost their job, couldn't make rent, and entire businesses 'disappeared.'

After seeing a post by a beloved small neighborhood bakery, openly sharing the financial devastation they were experiencing due to the COVID pandemic, Adam generously offered to use his 20+ years in eCommerce to help the bakery set up a way to sell their baked goods online. He was a light of hope and optimism in a time when all seemed dark.

Knowing that a thriving business was now worrying about surviving the week, he saw the writing on the wall. He understood that the issue expanded beyond his backyard. For every small local business he loved, there were untold numbers finding themselves in the same situation. Adam became the catalyst that brought people together so that action could be taken.

With the bakery already having offers of help from other people like Adam, a Mastermind was born. It was a gathering of people with varied, needed skills working toward a clearly defined purpose. Working together, they were able to launch purchasing online and delivery within days.

This is the power of a Mastermind.

Adam knew that countless other business owners were overwhelmed and didn't have the technical know-how, ability, or financial means to shift to an e-commerce model independently. So he called former colleagues, old friends, and even some fierce industry competitors that he felt would share his ambition and passion for making a difference. Within 24 hours, Adam assembled a Mastermind of ten leaders across various companies willing to offer their unique experience and expertise to help their local communities and small businesses. They partnered with different small businesses, saving them from permanently locking their doors.

Each member of the collective mastermind volunteered their time. Nobody was looking for profits or fame. They were genuinely looking to help. Every member was aligned emotionally and intellectually and there for the same reason. Their purpose was focused on a well-defined goal: change the course of as many small businesses as possible to support the owners and their employees across America.

Assembling a team was one thing. This mastermind thought the fastest way to make an impact was to make as many people as possible aware of WHY and HOW they should support their local small businesses. Letting them fail wasn't an option.

They needed to spread the word, and Adam knew exactly who to call. So when Adam reached out to me to let me know about the mastermind, I immediately asked how I could help. He and I were former colleagues, and as the founder and CEO of Voice Your Vibe, which hosted a global award- winning LIVE show about shouting out the good in the world, What's Good Wednesday (WGW), on LinkedIn, he knew it was a perfect fit and that I would be glad to help.

My expertise in digital marketing and live streaming was different from anyone in the group, and I have always had the mindset of helping and shining a light on others. The 100th episode of the show was coming up, and I told Adam I wanted to dedicate it to getting the word out about Keep Small Strong. WGW is seen in over 120 countries and featured on platforms such as IBM TV, Amazon Fire, LinkedIn LIVE, and RokuTV. So I knew I could provide the movement with the visibility it needed.

I was so strongly invested, intellectually and emotionally, that I asked the producer of my show if he would be willing to donate his time, knowledge, and skills. Like me, he was ready to help wherever he could.

The last step was letting people know about Keep Small Strong and shining the light on what they were doing.

While I was able to provide global digital visibility, our mastermind needed and was missing something else. I reached out to friends who wrote for globally respected national publications. They were experts in their field, and they, like each member, wanted to help. And so they wrote.

The mastermind met regularly, and communication was made through platforms reaching far and wide, with clear goals set, tasks distributed, and a well-oiled machine working together.

I had the honor and privilege of introducing Keep Small Strong to the world on my award-winning global weekly show, What's Good Wednesday. The hashtag, #KeepSmallStrong, launched live around the world, and the show featured multiple small business owners impacted by COVID-19 who shared their stories in their own words.

The mastermind encouraged everyone to spread the word to 'shop small' and find a small business to buy something from right away. So many people didn't know how critical it was for people to get to know how to find a small business and shop in their local stores to help the economy survive.

The mastermind purposely planned to simultaneously and strategically launch on Twitter, Instagram, and Facebook, and the website went live on the show (@KeepSmallStrong, and the KeepSmallStrong.org website). Any small business owner could now apply for assistance with online marketing and/or setting up an online storefront. Keep Small Strong also created a marketplace where small businesses could connect with their local communities and increase their brand exposure - regionally and nationally.

The mastermind knew that small businesses across America needed help fast, and they could make an impact together.

One member of the mastermind said it perfectly, "Those of us with the resources and ability to help should. It's our duty to protect and support those searching for answers. Whether that's a shoulder to lean on, an ear to bend, a bit of inspiration, or a shared tear, we're all in this together. Our goal is to help, guide, and inspire. If not us, then who? Lean in, ask questions, and share your story. We are listening."

Leucadia 101 was one of the small businesses that reached out to Keep Small Strong. It is an organization that relies on grants, income from events, and the generosity of the community in order to support local businesses with marketing and visibility.

What Leucadia 101 had been doing to raise funds to support businesses suddenly disappeared with the pandemic. Large, in-person events were no longer possible. Without the revenue generated, Leucadia 101 would have to close their doors, which would impact the businesses it supported.

Leucadia is an incredible town, and Leucadia 101 does such tremendous work to support small businesses in their community. And they needed help.

The mastermind created an event called LeucadiAID, which would be the organization's first-ever live-streaming benefit concert.

LeucadiAID, an online event, was created to raise funds in place of their traditional in-person events. They needed this to survive but weren't familiar with what it took to run virtual events. They had never done anything like this before. This is where my specialized knowledge of delivering LIVE shows and virtual events to a diverse global audience came in. Once again, I reached out to fellow experts in the live-streaming community and asked for help.

I was honored to host and produce this event. I pride myself on taking every opportunity to positively impact my community locally and globally.

Together, we organized a Run Of Show. The mastermind found 6 local Bands who volunteered their time, local businesses to donate their products to be sold to raise money, and sponsors were secured and were generous.

This event generated thousands of dollars and helped keep Leucadia101 Mainstreet alive, who were there to help keep their local businesses and families alive and thriving.

A Mastermind is only as strong as its weakest link. With a common goal, a positive attitude toward helping each other, expertise across multiple areas, goals distributed, and tasks accomplished, the power of a mastermind is unparalleled.

BRIAN SCHULMAN

About Brian Schulman: Known as the Godfather, and Pioneer, of LinkedIn Video and 1 of the world's premiere live streaming & video marketing experts, using a heart-centered, growth mindset while leveraging the power of LinkedIn's community and platform, Brian has transformed how business is conducted on LinkedIn worldwide. Founder & CEO of VoiceYourVibe, Brian brings his 20+ years experience, wealth of knowledge and proven Digital Marketing expertise, to Podcasters, Entrepreneurs, C-Suite Executives globally as an advisor and mentor through groundbreaking Masterminds, Workshops, 1-on-1 and Team Mastery Coaching.

Brian and Team work with clients strategically to build and increase strong brand recognition, grow your network, generate consistent, reliable revenue streams, and create a purpose-driven message that sets you apart from the ~1 billion business professionals on LinkedIn.

8X #1 Best-Selling Author and internationally known Keynote Speaker, Brian's expertise, insights & 2 Global Award-Winning LIVE Shows have been featured on NASDAQ, Forbes, Thrive Global, Yahoo Finance, Viacom, ROKU TV, The CW, multiple #1 best-selling books, syndicated on Smart TV Networks and hundreds of shows and podcasts, reaching millions world-wide.

Among his many awards and honors, Brian has been named a 'LinkedIn Top Voice', 'LinkedIn Video Creator Of The Year', 3X 'Top 50 Most Impactful People of LinkedIn' and 2X 'LinkedIn

Global Leader of The Year'. His 2 global award-winning weekly LIVE shows #ShoutOutSaturday & #WhatsGoodWednesday, broadcasted in 120+ countries, were named "Best LIVE Festive Show of The Year" at the IBM TV Awards.

Beyond the achievements and accolades, Brian is proudest of his 2 children and the relationships he's made along the way.

Author's Website: *www.VoiceYourVibe.com*
Book Series Website & Author's Bio: *www.The13StepsToRiches.com*

Candace & David Rose

STREAM OF POWER

"There exists in life a great unseen STREAM OF POWER which may be compared to a river—except that one side flows in one direction, carrying all who get into that side of the stream onward and upward to WEALTH, while the other side flows in the opposite direction, carrying all who are unfortunate enough to get into it (and not able to extricate themselves from it), downstream to misery and POVERTY."

~Napoleon Hill, Think and Grow Rich

"Gandhi… attained POWER through inducing more than 200 million people to cooperate, with mind and body, in a spirit of HARMONY, for a DEFINITE PURPOSE."

~Napoleon Hill, Think and Grow Rich

"A group of brains coordinated (or connected) in a spirit of harmony will provide more thought-energy than a single brain, just as a group of electric batteries will provide more energy than a single battery."

~Napoleon Hill, Think and Grow Rich

CANDACE & DAVID ROSE

About Candace and David Rose: Candace & David are #1 Best-Selling Authors in the book series, *The 13 Steps to Riches*. Candace and David grew up together and currently live in Alvarado, Texas with their Six Children, two Chickens, one Dog, four Cats and a rabbit. They both are veterans of the US Army. David, served as a mechanic and Candace as a Legal NCO. David is currently a Product Release Specialist, delivering Liquid Oxygen and Nitrogen to various manufacturing plants and hospitals throughout Texas. Candace specializes in helping people organize their space, both physically and mentally—with the ultimate goal to help you change your box and find more joy in your life. Both Candace and David are proud members of the elite Champion Circle Networking Association founded in Salt Lake City, UT, by one of our co-authors of *The 13 Steps To Riches* book series, Jon Kovach Jr.

Author's Website: *www.ChangeYourBox.com*
Book Series Website & Author's Bio: *www.The13StepsToRiches.com*

Corey Poirier

THE MASTERMIND

Of all of the universal laws in *Think and Grow Rich*, The Mastermind is the one I have practiced the most and seen the biggest results from.

I recall that I didn't fully understand what a mastermind was the first time I read *Think and Grow Rich*.

It was explained well enough, but I just couldn't visualize it in action and certainly couldn't understand why it was so powerful.

I didn't understand that there was a structure to masterminds and that they could yield tangible and intangible results.

I also didn't understand the relationships that could be built when multiple parties are joined in a regular group initiative like the mastermind.

After being a part of a few very short-term masterminds, I finally saw the power of multiple people coming together and working together toward a common goal.

As a result, I decided to take matters into my own hands and started my own mastermind. I brought together five people, including myself, and we decided we would meet weekly. Given the distance between our locations, we decided to begin meeting remotely.

In fact, I was the only person in the group who knew every member and am also the only one to meet almost every group member since.

We began our weekly mastermind almost seven years ago; we have had structure more on than off and have met weekly, other than a tiny number of breaks or moved meetings, since.

Basically, we did group discussions around a video or certain topic, did hotseats, shared resources, and even did a *Think and Grow Rich* book club.

80% of those first people who joined are still in the mastermind today, and we are still meeting weekly all these years later.

We've only had a few changes in all those years.

Since we began meeting, we've had personal conversations around health, wealth, loss, family, business successes and failures, personal successes and struggles, and more.

I've been able to rely on the members as my sounding board in launching my speaking program, which was a success in part thanks to their suggestions and feedback.

I've been able to launch books, programs, boot camps, and more, and while doing so have had an instant focus group to help me mold them into better offerings.

I've had people I felt I could be completely open with. I've had people who could refer me to certain resources, suppliers, and platforms that would have taken me countless hours to discover or connect with on my own.

And I've had four to five friends at all times that I could count on and who have my best interests at heart.

I only hope they can say the same about my part in their lives.

And that is the power of a mastermind: the richness and 'true' wealth it brings to my life. Now that I've had that experience, I truly can't imagine going alone.

I've also since joined other masterminds, some formal, some very informal, with varying degrees of success. I've also been able to contribute to many worthy causes due to being involved in these applicable masterminds.

One thing I like, and something I often think is overlooked when referring to masterminds, is Hill's take that when two people get together, a third mind, the Master Mind, is created.

I like this take because I believe in the case of The Mastermind, as Hill describes it, and as I have experienced it, that one and one do equal three.

Now, in being full disclosure here, I think the one thing missing from my mastermind groups, the one I created and the ones I have joined, though, is the idea of working together toward one very clear and common goal.

More often than not, the masterminds I have been a part of have involved things like hot seats, where each person shares their goals and struggles, etc. Then the other group members offer suggestions, feedback and support, resources, and so on, but we're not working toward a group or common goal.

I think the approach we take, where it involves multiple people, each running their own business, works exceptionally well. But, still, I truly would like to experience and explore the idea of working with someone, almost in a business partnership, or working with multiple people as part of a charitable foundation we start together so that we can work toward one common goal together.

I've been on boards and in various groups and masterminds, but that is the one thing that is always missing. Hill describes a key aspect of masterminds in the book concerning the power of masterminds: the idea that if two people work toward a common goal together, they have a much better chance of achieving that goal than each working on it alone.

And so, I guess that perhaps is my next step in the world of masterminding.

In the interim, though, I just want you to know that if you haven't masterminded yet, you should add it into the mix of what you do for your personal and business or professional life.

As noted, it's been such a big part of my life and the successes I've enjoyed. It's hard for me to envision myself having the life I have today without my mastermind experiences.

Oh, and my girlfriend of eight years has even watched our weekly mastermind become what it is today, has commented many times about how she sees me get so much from it, and is now a member.

I dare say that she would list our fellow masterminders among the people she trusts the most in this world, which alone is priceless.

The takeaway? I love masterminds, and I recommend them, and if you haven't masterminded yet, please give it a try. It might just change your life as it has mine.

COREY POIRIER

About Corey Poirier: Corey Poirier is a multiple-time TEDx Speaker. He is also the host of the top-rated '*Let's Do Influencing*' Radio Show, founder of the growing bLU Talks brand, and has been featured in multiple television specials. He is also a Barnes and Noble, Amazon, Apple Books, Kobo Bestselling Author, Award-Winning Author, and the co-author of the *Wall Street Journal* / USA Today Bestseller, *Quitless*.

A columnist with *Entrepreneur* and *Forbes* magazine, he has been featured in/on various mediums and is one of the few leaders featured twice on the popular Entrepreneur on Fire show.

He has also interviewed over 6,500 of the world's top leaders, and he has spoken on-site at Harvard and Columbia University, and more recently to Microsoft team leaders and at Kyle Wilson's Inner Circle retreat, which has featured everyone from Brian Tracy to Mark Victor Hansen to Phil Collen (Def Leppard).

Also appearing on the popular Evan Carmichael YouTube Channel, he is a New Media Summit Icon of Influence, was recently listed as the # 5 Influencer in Entrepreneurship by Thinkers 360, and listed on the 2021 Brainz CREA Global Awards as an honoree, and he is a Humanitarian Hero Award Nominee, Entrepreneur of the Year Nominee, Champion Award (Business from The Heart) nominee, and to demonstrate his versatility, a Rock Recording of the Year Nominee who has performed stand-up comedy more than 700 times, including an appearance at the famed Second City.

Author's Website: *www.TheInfluencerVault.com*
Book Series Website & Author's Bio: *www.The13StepsToRiches.com*

Deb Scott

POWER OF THE MASTER OF MIND: THE DRIVING FORCE

"Power is essential for the success in the accumulation of money."

Napoleon Hill talks about Power needing to be translated into action. Hill defines Power as "organized and intelligently directed knowledge."

Hill states, "power is required for the accumulation of money: power is necessary for the retention of money after it has been accumulated."

Hill acknowledges that power may be acquired by:
1. Infinite Intelligence
2. Accumulated experience
3. Experiment and Research

As in previous chapters, the core of any plan is action, and without action, nothing can be accomplished.

The Master Mind is a hinge that can open this door more easily. Surrounding yourself with a group of people willing to share their wisdom, creative ideas, and personal experience as to how they achieved their goals is imperative.

Hill recognizes that everything is energy, including the mind. By surrounding yourself with this part of a living energy and spirit, you can naturally attract some of this "psychic" knowledge and power into your mind. "A group of electric batteries will provide more energy than a single battery."

In my own best-selling book, *"The Sky is Green and the Grass is Blue – turning your upside-down world right side up!"* I had an entire chapter about using seminars and retreats as a way to gain this power of the collective energy source of success easily and in a fun manner.

Just like when you spray perfume on yourself, it naturally sends its scent to everything surrounding the path nearby.

You can watch a baseball game on tv or go to the stadium and experience it live with thousands of other people focused on the same event. You are watching the game in both situations, but which one is giving you the greatest experience of energy, insight, and power? Of course, being at the event live with the thousands of others who joined you to participate in the same goal.

Power is something that will come to you through surrounding yourself with people who already have what you want.

If you desire to be a pro tennis player, do you take lessons from the worst or best tennis player you can find? Obtaining wealth, success, happiness, and your goals and dreams is no different.

Hill also speaks of the need to visualize, meditate, the obtain your desire of having your riches. He is not being religious, but he is stating faith is necessary to materialize what is spiritual into material.

The mind scientifically does not recognize the difference between a thought in your imagination vs. an actual event. Studies show that looking at pictures of people doing acts of kindness produces the same amount of feel-good endorphins as if you were doing the act of kindness yourself.

According to the International Coaching Academy's neuroscience and visualization research paper, an idea over and over [in your mind], your brain will begin to respond as though the idea was a real object in the world.

"The thalamus [the part of the reality-making process of the brain] makes no distinction between inner and outer realities, and thus, **any idea, if contemplated long enough, will take on a semblance of reality** *... The concept begins to feel more attainable and real, and this is the first step in motivating other parts of the brain to take deliberate action in the world."*

In my own life, I visualized during major snowstorms in the Boston area living near a palm tree with the warm sunshine soothing my body and soul. I visualized the beach and a happy community where I would be peaceful. I had never heard of Venice, Florida, nor had I ever been to Venice. Yet somehow, that visualization transformed into reality, and here I am under the palm trees in the most lovely town in South West Florida by the gulf coast.

"Brain studies now reveal that thoughts produce the same mental instructions as actions. Mental imagery impacts many cognitive processes in the brain: motor control, attention, perception, planning, and memory. So, the brain is getting trained for actual performance during visualization. It's been found that mental practices can enhance motivation, increase confidence and self- efficacy, improve motor performance, prime your brain for success, and increase states of flow— all relevant to achieving your best life!" ~ Psychology Today.

"Begin by establishing a highly specific goal. Imagine the future; you have already achieved your goal. Hold a mental "picture" of it as if it were occurring to you right at that moment. Imagine the scene in as much detail as possible. Engage as many of the five senses as you can in your visualization. Who are you with? Which emotions are you feeling right now? What are you wearing? Is there a smell in the air? What do you hear?

What is your environment? Sit with a straight spine when you do this. Practice at night or in the morning (just before/after sleep). Eliminate any doubts if they come to you. Repeat this practice often. Combine with meditation or an affirmation (e.g., "I am courageous; I am strong," or to borrow from Ali, "I am the greatest!").

I visualize speaking and teaching around the world about how to "sell without selling" because, having been a salesperson all my career, I really don't care much for salespeople. Instead, I care about people and relationships. When the world focuses on service, integrity, sharing knowledge, and being an honest source of high-quality information people can trust, sales will come naturally.

In my career in medical sales, writing a best-selling book, having an award-winning podcast, owning a small vintage boutique, or even now in real estate, I have been blessed to be an award winner in each of these throughout my life. I have been consistently at the top of sales or awards for excellence, not because I was focused on the money first but because the outcome of helping people genuinely find value in my service and support is the best beyond measure. This motivates me most personally, so this was my focus and diligent plan to accomplish through faith, desire, action, and all the items Napoleon Hill lists in his book. The money always followed. In that order.

Believing in the power of your unique gifts and talents is imperative because if you don't believe in yourself, it is impossible to expect anyone else to. Visualization and surrounding yourself with others who have what you want will catapult you much faster to achieve your goals because we all need each other in this world.

"Anybody can wish for riches, and most people do, but only a few know that a definite plan, a burning desire for wealth, are the only dependable means of actuating wealth." ~ Napoleon Hill

DEB SCOTT

About Deb Scott: Deb Scott, BA, CPC, and Realtor was a high honors biology major at Regis College in Weston, Massachusetts, and spent over two decades as an award-winning cardio-thoracic sales specialist in the New England area. She is a best-selling author of *The Sky is Green & The Grass is Blue: Turning Your Upside Down World Right Side Up.* She is an award-winning podcaster of The Best People We Know Show. Following in her family's footsteps, she is a third generation Realtor in Venice, Florida. As a certified life coach, Deb speaks and teaches on how to turn bad situations into positive, successful results. As a top sales specialist, she enjoys teaching people "sales without selling," believing that integrity, good communication, and respect are the winning equation to all outstanding success and happiness in life.

Author's Website: *www.DebScott.com*

Book Series Website & Author's Bio: *www.The13StepsToRiches.com*

Dori Ray

POWER ON PURPOSE

"GREAT POWER CAN BE ACCUMULATED THROUGH NO OTHER PRINCIPLE THAN THAT OF THE MASTER MIND!"

~Napoleon Hill, Think And Grow Rich

"POWER IS ESSENTIAL FOR SUCCESS IN THE ACCUMULATION OF MONEY."

~Napoleon Hill, Think And Grow Rich

"WE MAKE A LIVING BY WHAT WE GET, BUT WE MAKE A LIFE BY WHAT WE GIVE."

~Winston Churchill

DORI RAY

About Dori Ray: Dori "On Purpose" Ray is a native Philadelphian. As a businesswoman, her mission is to help people transform their minds, bodies, and bank accounts!

Dori was educated in the Philadelphia Public School System. She graduated from the Philadelphia High School for Girls in 1982 and Howard University School of Business in 1986 with a BBA in Marketing. Dori is a member of Delta Sigma Pi Business Fraternity and Delta Sigma Theta Sorority, Inc.

Dori leads teams around the world. She is a sought-after Speaker and Trainer within her industry and beyond. She is an experienced Re-Entry Coach who has helped hundreds of Returning Citizens get back on track after incarceration.

Having suffered from depression for 20 years, she always reaches back to share her story and help break the cycle of silence. Her audience loves her authenticity! Book Dori for speaking engagements with her information below.

Author's Website: *www.linktr.ee/DoriOnPurpose*
Book Series Website & Author's Bio: *www.The13StepsToRiches.com*

Elaine Sugimura

MASTERMINDING YOUR WAY TO THE PINNACLE!

What does the word Powerful mean to you? What comes up for you when I ask that question? To be the Leader I have set out to become, I want and get to BE Powerful every second, minute, hour, and day of my life. It means having the courage, confidence, and commitment to do what it takes to be successful. But does success only arrive when we act alone? I would love to share my love of sports, thus the analogies and inspirational quotes supporting my climb up the mountain. Just thinking about this gives me goosebumps.

In the prior chapters in *The 13 Steps to Riches* book series, I referenced the distinctions from having a burning desire, faith, and infinite imagination to being organized and having the specialized knowledge to reach the pinnacle of success. These distinctions play a huge role in how one can achieve success. Let's define how power may be acquired. From my point of view, one way to obtain power is to have the keen knowledge to cause and create what you want to see as the result. So, let me share where this knowledge is sourced from:

Source 1: Having Infinite Intelligence that is supported by your and others' Creative Imagination.

Source 2: A Wealth of Experiences – what you have learned over your life and how to share it with others.

Source 3:   When the knowledge from sources 1 and 2 is unavailable, we get to dig deeper and be open to curiosity (Creative imagination) and further research.

Source 4:   ME, YOU, and OTHERS! In other words, TEAM!

When I accumulate knowledge from the sources above and through my experiences, I have learned what it takes to actually give and receive Power as a source for success. Converting knowledge into power requires being organized and having the definiteness of plans that must then be placed into distinct committed action. Once I grasped this, I knew that to successfully climb up the mountain, knowing it was steep and treacherous, would require more than my efforts alone. Thus, gaining the ultimate power and success meant being inclusive with others and asking them to be a part of the team. Through the Power of the Mastermind, it can be assumed that the coordination of effort, knowledge, and connection would achieve the overall strategy/plan. Over the years, this drove the success of many of the businesses I led and managed. It was threading the golden needle, which meant that, at all times, the context and content had to be managed throughout the project and plan.

I learned early on that success can only be achieved when power is present. When a definite purpose is known, power is acquired from a group of individuals. This results in a team that is charged at a different amplitude. Think about the voltage it takes to run an electrical appliance. If you use a lower voltage, the power is diminished, or the appliance may not work at all. Once you use the proper voltage, the power is sufficient. What I found to be more powerful is when the amplitude increases in humans (meaning more minds within the mastermind group), you will have a supercharged reaction and result. What I learned is lone-wolfing will only get you so far with your strategy/plan. This quote comes to mind as I am speaking about TEAM.

"Individuals merely score; TEAMS WIN!"

~ Jay Margolis

I mentioned in prior chapters that sports analogies really land for me. To WIN at a team sport that you choose to play requires that you not only learn to play the game but also to be a part of the team. The team must be willing to take instruction from the coach as they have been hired for one sole purpose—TO WIN THE GAME. So, take a moment and take that in. If the coach is hired to WIN the game, what do each of the players get to bring to the game? If everyone who played or plays the game of basketball as Michael Jordan did, what would the outcome be? As I reflect on this possibility, it energizes me in a way that brings forth opportunity, unbridled focus, positive energy, a winning mindset, team, inclusion, joy, happiness, and inspiration. So, what did it take Michael Jordan to WIN 6 NBA Championships? After watching his Netflix documentary, *The Last Dance*, we learned that he was willing to leave it all on the court. He never requested of his teammates what he was unwilling to do himself. His DESIRE to be the MVP and be the best team that ever played the game of basketball was what drove his persistence to perfect not only his mind but also his body. When the two were on the same page, so to speak, everything rang up as SUCCESS! And when you include that his teammates were willing to stretch themselves to a new level and have the best mind and body, this points to their definiteness of strategy/plan that rewarded them with championship wins. This is a mastermind of its own. You see, to be the best of the best requires multiple minds that are focused on the same strategy/plan and goal. Once this is achieved, the pinnacle is reached!

After reading my words thus far, you must think I have it all together. On the contrary, please note that achieving success did not happen every day or every year of my life. I, too, am human and have made mistakes, fallen prey to disappointment, procrastination, sadness, and even felt like giving up. But I knew that to reinvent or transform how I approached all I was responsible for meant knowing that Knowledge is Power. Anything and everything was possible through my fierce persistence, creative imagination, uber commitment, and, ultimately, a huge dose of courage. It meant knowing that quitting was never an option. So, when we couple our absolute burning desire with the definiteness of a strategy/plan, we inspire others to be a part of the winning strategy. This was my formula for success. By being inclusive, open, and curious about what possibilities were available, there was more than the "hope" that the strategy/plan would work. Persistence breeds persistence! Success is Contagious! By consistently being in committed and distinct action, there was no time to worry about the negative thoughts or influences that were always lurking as there were always those who were either in competition and/or wanted to see the team or myself fail. I truly learned to embrace the fact that failure creates mastery! And when masterful minds get together, anything and everything is possible!

So, strap your bootstraps on real tight and take the mastermind ride of your LIFE. Know that the past is the past, and the only time we have is the moment we are in NOW and the FUTURE. So, clap your hands and say, "New Moment," and see the blank canvas that lies before you and begin to paint the picture you want to see in front of you. Your strategy/plan is already in front of you so remind yourself that every moment is a CHOICE moment, and you have multiple possibilities and opportunities. Choose the possibility that best aligns with the success and definiteness of your strategy/plan, and you will experience success. Remember, you do not all have to agree, but as long as everyone has a vote, you can align on what is best for the overall group. Be flexible, be ease and flow and when you surrender and trust yourself and others, what do you believe is possible? I will answer that for you. You will experience expansion, abundance, freedom, inspiration, and success! Now that is what I call a winning mastermind formula that will, undoubtedly, take you to the pinnacle of success!

I want to leave you with what Napoleon Hill shared regarding the Power of the Mastermind...

> *"The Master Mind Principle: Two or more people actively engaged in the pursuit of a definite purpose with a positive mental attitude constitute an unbeatable force."* ~ Napoleon Hill

Lastly, remember that we can cause and create what we want in our lives. This is what responsibility is at its highest level. Life is meant to be lived in the present. LIFE is NOW. If that is true, then this quote summarizes what we have been speaking about.

> *"Alone, we can do so little. Together we can do so much."*
> ~ Helen Keller

ELAINE SUGIMURA

About Elaine R. Sugimura: Elaine is an accomplished CEO turned Business Consultant / Life Strategist who has a passion to create Leaders amongst Leaders. With over 35+ years in the fashion and food and beverage industry, she has a passion to not only lead but support those who are seeking to reinvent who they are no matter where they are in life. She is a two-time breast cancer survivor and she knows a thing or two about surviving to thriving. Fun fact: she is an adrenaline junkie—the higher, the faster, the better. Her love for adventure has led her to travel to many parts of the world by plane, train and automobile. She and her husband, Hiro, share their home in Northern California. They have raised two extraordinary sons, Bryce and Cole and have added two beautiful daughters-in-law, Erica and Giselle to their growing family. Her legacy is to share what is possible when we open ourselves up to the issues that hold us back. Her Life's mission is to move those who are just surviving into Thrivers!

Author's Website: *www.ElaineRSugimura.com*
Book Series Website & Author's Bio: *www.The13StepsToRiches.com*

Elizabeth Anne Walker

THE DRIVING FORCE BEHIND A TRUE MASTERMIND

A tiny water droplet formed at the end of a eucalyptus leaf on the dawn of a spectacular Australian morning. It glistened in the sun as the sound of birdsong from Butcher birds and Currawongs filled the air. The heat of the sun was barely present, and, apart from the melodic tune, the earth was still. The tiny droplet watched the sky change colors through a spectacular dance of light. Grey through purple, then orange, and finally yellow into a perfect blue sky. The drop was in awe. It looked around, and there seemed to be no one else there. The birds hadn't noticed the droplet, and it seemed such a shame that such beauty was unable to be shared.

As the day continued to awaken, the sky filled with light, and the birds flew. The scream of cicadas filled the air, and the little droplet began to wonder what the day would hold and, distracted in thought, felt a sense of sliding. Down, down, down, and then the fear set in; what's happening to me? Where am I going? What is this?

The warmth had allowed the droplet to slide all the way down the leaf and land in a puddle on the floor below. The droplet was dazed at first, and noticed that it was surrounded by other droplets in the puddle, some were moving, and some were still. Of those moving, some appeared engrossed in activity, and others seemed to stand and chat about not much at all. The little droplet was so excited! There are others like me!

The droplet wandered around and saw that, where the droplets were in activity and talking together at the same time, there was even more movement! A sense of flow even! The little droplet got excited and joined a moving group, and life began to flow! The flow was slow at first, but as each new droplet joined the movement, the flow sped up!

At first, it was just movement in the puddle, and over time as more and more droplets joined and shared the stories of their journey of how they got into the puddle, the flow started. There was movement back and forward at first, and then slowly but surely, the large puddle and the drops within it started their journey away from the tree.

Pushing, expanding, and forward momentum, the droplets became more and more excited as it happened. They started doing more things as they tumbled over the bushland floor. The smell of eucalypt beneath them, the canopy above them, the movement was real. And at first, it seemed like the droplets at the front were pulling the droplets at the back. Then, finally, they entered a creek bed with a sandy floor, and it seemed to slow down for a moment. And then suddenly, from behind, a surge occurred, momentum reignited, and along the creek bed, they flowed. There were some turns and twists where they momentarily slowed down and some turns with a speed that was overwhelming and very exciting.

The little droplet reflected and thought about how it was so great to share this journey, remembering his time at dawn alone with no one to share in the beauty. He now had a whole creek to share the beauty with him. As more and more droplets joined from the trees and the rain that dribbled into the creek, the droplet realized that even if he wanted to, there was no way to stop now. And the great thing about that was that had he been alone, there were a few times in the creek where he found himself in a pool of deep stagnant water where he might have quit.

The creek rushed on and soon became a wide, beautiful, expansive, ever-moving river. The little droplet had created so much more than was ever imagined possible when sitting on that leaf all that time ago. So many sunrises had been seen, many animals had come to drink at the banks, many plants had been watered, and the droplet was well aware of the impact that had been created.

The river flowed faster as the banks narrowed to squeeze through and around suburbia and into the city. The lights were bright, and the little droplet knew exactly what its capabilities now were. And as well as being aware of the impact created, the droplet was aware of everything personally gained. There were friends, family, travel, and all the things a droplet could need. While speeding excitedly through the city, more droplets joined from the gutters, roads, and pathways and from the drains of human homes. And every time a droplet joined, the original droplet was so excited because every morning, there was someone to share that sunrise with, and every evening there was someone to share the sunset with. So the beauty of the world was shared in a way that everyone got to enjoy it.

Out of the city and the expanse came again as the river mouth opened and saw the droplet become one with the ocean. The driving force of all the other droplets had taken him on a journey that had prepared him to feel at peace in the world's largest expanse of water. Here in the wild ocean, the momentum was undeniable. It was ever moving and changing; what was under it, the sand, and over it, the sky, was also moving and changing all the time.

The droplet enjoyed the ocean, all the creatures, and the vast array of birds. The constant movement, the pull from the moon creating the tides, the waves dancing in the depths and crashing on the shore. It wasn't always pleasant, yet the droplet loved it all. The droplet felt complete and knew that time on this beautiful earth was finite. The droplet had experienced everything life had to offer, had created impacts far wider than initially imagined, and had created a movement the other droplets could enjoy and become a part of.

On a hot summer day in a beautiful tropical ocean, surrounded by islands and a warm, slow breeze, palm trees, and white sand visible on the horizon, the droplet felt a pull that hadn't been felt before. He had heard about the pull, yet this was the first time the feeling had ever been present.

The pull was real and became stronger and stronger, and the droplet realized it was ascending out of the ocean. At first, it was exciting, and the droplet felt other droplets behind him. Lifting, lifting, lifting into the air, the droplet looked around and saw the most beautiful tropical panoramic vista. Then the feeling came again, that feeling of loneliness, and as the droplet looked upon himself, he realized he'd changed. He didn't look the same anymore; in fact, he didn't even recognize himself. All the momentum, all the creation, all the movement, had changed him. And as he looked back at the ocean, he realized he was different, and while he felt alone, it wasn't nearly as scary this time.

He rose up, up into the air, and he noticed other droplets were rising too, although they all seemed to be going it alone again. He wasn't sad; he was proud. He knew the ocean had been part of his creation and could always be grateful for that. While he had no idea where he was going, he had the certainty that all he had to do when he arrived was find those like him who were in movement and taking action and join them to reignite the flow.

The droplet arrived high in the sky, and when he introduced himself as a droplet, everyone there told him his new identity was vapor. He realized he could gain energy from the ether!

And as he realized how to harness this energy, he also realized he could translate energy into matter. And the impact he had previously provided him the skills to move to the next creation. He joined a cloud where others were taking action, translating energy into matter, and started on his next creative project. Over and over again, he created, and the view from above was both inspiring and uplifting. He realized he had influence over so many of the projects below.

Once he was satisfied his masterpiece from this position was created, he leaned back, satisfied with his work. Right at that moment, he experienced gratitude, and the journey started again as he became rain that fell onto the ground, evaporated onto a leaf, and fell into a puddle. What an incredible journey.

ELIZABETH WALKER

About Elizabeth Walker: Elizabeth is Australia's leading Female Integrated NLP Trainer, an international speaker with Real Success, and the host of Success Resources's (Australia's largest and most successful events promoter, including speakers such as Tony Robbins and Sir Richard Branson) inaugural Australian Women's Program "The Seed." Elizabeth has guided many people to achieve complete personal breakthroughs and phenomenal personal and business growth. With over 25 years of experience transforming the lives of hundreds of thousands of people, Elizabeth's goal is to assist leaders to create the reality they choose to live, impacting millions on a global scale.

A thought leader who has worked alongside people like Gary Vaynerchuck, Kerwin Rae, Jeffery Slayter, and Kate Gray, Elizabeth has an outstanding method of delivering heart with business.

As a former lecturer in medicine at the University of Sydney and lecturer in nursing at Western Sydney University, Elizabeth was instrumental in the research and development of the stillbirth and neonatal death pathways, ensuring each family in Australia went home knowing what happened to their child, and felt understood, heard, and seen.

A former Australian Champion in Trampolining and Australian Dance sport, Elizabeth has always been passionate about the mindset and skills required to create the results you are seeking.

Author's website: *www.ElizabethAnneWalker.com*
Book Series Website & Author's Bio: *www.The13StepsToRiches.com*

Erin Ley

TEAMWORK MAKES THE DREAM WORK

Napoleon Hill brilliantly states in his classic book from 1937, *Think and Grow Rich*, "The psychic phase of the Master Mind principle is much more abstract, much more difficult to comprehend because it has reference to the spiritual forces with which the human race, as a whole, is not well acquainted. You may catch a significant suggestion from this statement: 'No two minds ever come together without, thereby, creating a third, invisible, intangible force which may be likened to a third mind.' Keep in mind that there are only two known elements in the universe, energy, and matter. It is a well-known fact that matter may be broken down into units of molecules, atoms, and electrons. There are units of matter which may be isolated, separated, and analyzed. Likewise, there are units of energy. The human mind is a form of energy, a part of it being spiritual in nature. When the minds of two people are coordinated in a spirit of harmony, each mind's spiritual units of energy form an affinity, which constitutes the 'psychic' phase of the Master Mind."

And this is where miracles start to happen! Accomplishments happen at record speed! My father has a Ph.D. in philosophy. I've had really deep conversations with my father for as far back as I can remember. I used to joke with him that I'm probably one of the few that can follow his conversations from A-Z. I'd go on to say that many people probably checked out at D-E-or-F. I love my conversations with my father. I'd challenge his position.

We'd debate certain fundamental existential philosophical beliefs. And at the end of the conversation, I felt a deeper connection with myself and my father. I knew that I could deepen the conversation others were having with themselves. My father and I had our own private Master Mind when discussing his or my goals. Epiphanies happened. Insights were born.

I took this knowledge with me when I entered the workplace in my early twenties on Wall Street. I sat in meetings and looked forward to those in the room sharing experience, insight, and wisdom to form the best decision on a common goal. Through clarity and counsel, we'd Master Mind.

Napoleon Hill defines the Master Mind as the "Coordination of knowledge and effort, in a spirit of harmony, between two or more people, for the attainment of a definite purpose."

When I was in my mid-twenties, I began to Master Mind with my doctors. I was diagnosed with non-Hodgkin's lymphoblastic lymphoma in 1991. I knew I needed "smart council," wisdom from those who knew best. I met with many doctors, insurance agents, nurses, and those who thought they were going to tell me what to do and what was in my best interest; however, I had the background and the insight that most did not have. The intuition I had far surpassed many of the professionals I encountered. As I spoke with many in the professional realm, I understood who knew more than others. I knew it was imperative to shop around for the appropriate medical care and make sure those in charge of my care were open to masterminding with me instead of just telling me what to do. I needed to know not only what they were going to do regarding my medical plan and treatment but also why they were doing it. I craved a full understanding of what was going on and needed to be part of the decision-making process. If there was something I did not understand, the medical team explained it to me. We came together in a spirit of harmony whereby my ultimate restoration of health and well-being was the definite purpose.

After my protocol was over in the mid-1990s, and after I defied death more than once during the two-and-a-half-year protocol, I went on to have three miracle children that the doctors swore I would never have. The doctors and I continued to Master Mind. Then the doctors at Memorial Sloan-Kettering Cancer Center began to have their patients call me at home. They could not explain what I was doing when defying the negative odds, so they had me Master Mind with their patients. I became clear on what their needs were and what the definite purpose was for every call. I provided counsel based on my experience. It was hard-earned wisdom as opposed to opinion. When I told the doctors I could not take the calls anymore from the cancer patients because I felt like I was neglecting my three miracle children by spending so much time on the phone, the doctors said I shouldn't stop and that I should be doing this for a living. They said their patients had a new outlook on life, and many were no longer getting sick from chemotherapy and radiation treatments. They said I am an amazing Life Coach and should be setting appointments. I asked them what a Life Coach was. It was the nineties, and Life Coaching was new. When this one doctor explained what Life Coaching was, I began my own practice and have enjoyed it ever since. Masterminding with my cancer patients, inspiring, and empowering them was what I felt called to do back then. These days I feel called to inspire and empower female entrepreneurs.

I remember being in Clubhouse last year with John Assaraf. John was in the movie *The Secret* and is brilliant in quantum physics. He wrote the book, *Innercise: The New Science to Unlock Your Brain's Hidden Power*. This book says that the latest brain science delivers the answers you need to break free and unlock the hidden power of your subconscious mind so you can earn more, live more, and achieve more than ever before. The time I spent in the same Clubhouse rooms with John felt like I was back in school, and I wanted to sit next to my friend because he understood me. John and I spoke passionately about quantum physics and the miracles that can happen because we understand what this is all about. What my father studied as part of his Ph.D. in philosophy and went on later to teach after retiring from a very successful career in the corporate world as a professor at St. John's University in philosophy was metaphysics. The difference between quantum physics and metaphysics is that quantum physics is science while metaphysics is philosophy. Quantum physics is the branch of physics that is concerned with things that take place at the subatomic scale. Metaphysics is the branch of philosophy that is concerned with the nature of reality. Both are such a gift and a blessing to understand at any age in life.

When I joined Erik Swanson's Habitude Warrior Mastermind, my business took off in miraculous ways. I was a single mom with three kids and now growing my business because I had to. It was difficult and very lonely. Once I joined the Habitude Warrior Mastermind and showed up for every meeting for my own clarity and counsel regarding my business, or I received what Erik calls borrowed benefits from someone else's clarity and counsel, my life began to take shape in such a beautiful way at record speed. I tapped into quantum physics, and I could see the stress melting from my face.

I began attracting ideal clients, and my private one-on-one Life Coaching practice developed a waiting list. I have a full practice as a Life Coach and Business Strategist, coaching individuals and business owners on overcoming the feeling of being stuck, in fear, or distracted to becoming focused, fearless, and excited about life. I do a lot of mindset work with my clients, and we Master Mind with their definite purpose as the end goal. I help my clients gain the clarity, confidence, and prosperity they deserve to live full lives with inner peace. I've developed the Life On Track in-person conference so this message that you can do, be, and have anything goes out to many more.

These days I'm called to empower female entrepreneurs to be all they can be through my Life On Track (personally and professionally) books, coaching, course, corporate workshops, tv show, online summits, and in-person conferences.

There's an old proverb, "If you want to go fast, go alone. If you want to go far, go with a team." I've never been happier, healthier, and wealthier than I am these days. I credit the work I do around having a crystal-clear vision, knowing exactly what I want in life personally and professionally, in conjunction with the clarity and counsel received in the Habitude Warrior Mastermind. All of it culminating in happiness and success while walking in faith and having the drive to constantly create to live life onward and upward.

ERIN LEY

About Erin Ley: As Founder and CEO of Onward Productions, Inc., Erin Ley has spent the last 30 years as an Author, Professional Speaker, Personal and Professional Empowerment and Success Coach predominantly around mindset, Vision and Decision. Founder of many influential summits, including "Life On Track," Erin is also the host of the upcoming online streaming T.V. Show "Life On Track with Erin Ley," which is all about helping you get into the driver's seat of your own life.

They call Erin "The Miracle Maker!" As a cancer survivor at age 25, single mom of 3 at age 47, successful Entrepreneur at age 50, Erin has shown thousands upon thousands across the globe how to become victorious by being focused, fearless, and excited about life and your future! Erin says, "Celebrate life and you'll have a life worth celebrating!"

To see more about Erin and the release of her 4th book "WorkLuv: A Love Story" along with her "Life On Track" Course & Coaching Programs, please visit her website.

Author's website: *www.ErinLey.com*
Book Series Website & Author's Bio: *www.The13StepsToRiches.com*

Fatima Hurd

MASTER THE MIND

It was late. I was ready for bed but received a test message from my friend Julie to hop on to the clubhouse app. I had just logged off, and being on that app was consuming my life. I was on it all the time! But I couldn't help it; I was seeking something; I was on there with a purpose.

Well, that night, Feb 23rd, 2021, little did I know my life would be changed. I decided to get back on the app. I went to the room she invited me to, where the host Erik Swanson was asking his guests to give their elevator pitches and explain what collaboration meant to them.

As soon as I entered the room, I was brought up to speak, and I was at a loss for words. This was the first time I really thought about my pitch. After moving to California in 2017 and closing the doors to my studio, I took a break from my photography.

When it was my turn, I was at a loss, and I did not have a pitch, nor had I thought about it in a while. Stumped and stumbling over words, Erik picked up on it and offered to help. Erik asked me to reach out the next day. I was nervous, and it had been a while, well over a couple of years, since I had done anything with my business. I had the occasional photo shoot that I did for friends, but other than that, I was far from running an actual business.

I got in touch with Erik the next day. He invited me to his Habitude Warrior Mastermind. I wasn't sure what to expect, but I was ready for whatever God had in store for me. Apparently, God had Erik in store for me.

Although I had read *Think & Grow Rich* many years before, I had forgotten about the Mastermind. That was the very first time I was ever invited to a mastermind. I was nervous as I looked around and saw all the professionals that filled up the squares on my screen.

This was very structured and very helpful. I knew I was exactly where I needed to be. The next day I was asked back to help as a team member. I accepted the best decision ever. This changed the direction of my life, and I experienced so many possibilities of being among the great minds of such an incredible community of like-minded individuals.

Six months later, I officially started my photography business back up and pivoted to Personal Branding Photography. I knew then that I wanted to work with entrepreneurs.

After being on the team for about a year, I decided to join as an actual member. I quickly realized the benefits that came with being a member, and for me having 100% of my attention on the conversations that were being had, such immense value that I didn't want to be distracted by the duties that came with being a team member. Some people are great at multitasking, but I was not one of them. I knew if I wanted to take advantage of the full benefits of this MASTERMIND, I needed to be a member. So I resigned and became a paid member and never looked back.

The other benefits of being part of such an incredible community were the connections/friendships I made with the other members. Being part of this MASTERMIND opened up so much for me. It opened up a world of possibilities.

It's been a year and a half since I met Erik and joined his mastermind. Since then, I have become an eight time #1 best-selling author. My business has grown, and I had the opportunity to meet some of our amazing celebrity authors, thanks to Mr. Swanson, aka Mr. Awesome.

Being part of this mastermind has expanded my knowledge, network, and desire to be the best version of myself. I love Erik's motto, "NDSO, No Drama Serve Others."

I love this so much because it resonates with me so well. I love helping and supporting others as well. It was usually a one-way street in the past, but being part of this mastermind, I realized I had found my people. I found people who share the same values I do, helping each other so that we all rise together.

The benefits of being part of the Habitude Warrior Mastermind that was created under the principles of *Think & Grow Rich* are far more than I could ever imagine. Sounding myself with other professionals who have experience and are more than willing to share what has worked for them has helped me immensely in building my business.

I love that I can also contribute what has worked for me. And that my experience can help others in their business as well.

In *Think & Grow Rich*, Napoleon Hill says, "People take on the nature and the habits and the POWER OF THOUGHT of those with whom they associate in a spirit of sympathy and harmony."

I know in my heart that I wouldn't be where I am today if I wouldn't follow through on the opportunity offered to me by Erik to join his mastermind.

However, joining the mastermind is only part of it. I feel the following steps are what have brought me so much success:

- Being coachable. I went all in when I decided to join, almost like a child-like wonder, ready to learn and be open.
- Listen! This skill is vital, and I had to build this muscle when it came to listening. To help others, you must listen to what they are saying. You must really listen, and to reap the benefits of being part of the mastermind, you must also listen to the feedback you are getting.
- As I heard before, knowledge is not power if it is not followed with action. You can read all the books you want and learn so much, but it's pointless if you don't take action. It's just taking up space.
- Gratitude! Coming in with a heart filled with gratitude for being part of such a beautiful space with great minds.
- Investing in yourself is key to your exponential growth. Before joining my first mastermind, I found it very difficult to spend my hard earn money on courses, training, or anything that promised I would make me million dollars. But having had the opportunity to join the mastermind first as a team member helped me see the true value of the mastermind and how investing in it was worth every penny. There were no regrets or guilt.

Since then, I have been invited to many other masterminds, and they are different. But Habitude Warrior Mastermind will always be my home, my community that holds a special place in my heart. It changed my life! For me, masterminds are all about mastering the mind through subtle shifts and habits that help you improve your life through borrowed benefits from those you surround yourself with. As they say, you are who you hang out with.

So who are you hanging out with? Do they bring value to your life, and do you add value to theirs?

FATIMA HURD

About Fatima Hurd: Fatima is a personal brand photographer and was featured in the special edition of Beauty & Lifestyle's mommy magazine. Fatima specializes in personal branding photographs dedicated to helping influencers and entrepreneurs expand their reach online with strategic, creative, inspiring, and visual content. Owner of a digital consulting agency, Social Branding Digital Solutions, Fatima helps professionals with all their digital needs.

Fatima holds ten years of photography experience. An expert in her field, she hosts workshops to teach anyone who wants to learn how to use and improve their skills with DSLR and on manual mode. Hurd is also a mother of three, wife, certified Reiki master, and certified crystal healer. She loves being out in nature, enjoys taking road trips with her family, and loves meditation and yoga on the beach.

Author's website: *www.FatimaHurd.com*
Book Series Website & Author's Bio: *www.The13StepsToRiches.com*

Frankie Fegurgur

MAY I BORROW YOUR BRAIN?

When most people hear the word 'mastermind,' it conjures images of the quintessential evil villain amid sinister plans for world domination. Of course, I don't mean that kind of mastermind. However, it's still a useful reference for exploring the ego and how we interpret our experiences. In the case of works of fiction, if there is a villain, there must also be a hero. The hero is perceived as the antithesis of the villain, but a closer examination reveals a more complicated narrative. The hero and villain often share similar origin stories. Typically, they experienced a tragedy in their youth, such as the loss of a loved one or an unforgivable betrayal. So why does one character descend to wickedness while the other fights for justice?

The villain and the hero of any story choose differently. The difference between the manipulative, cruel villain and the honorable, revered hero is intention. The villain chose selfishness, ego, and the belief that the ends justify the means. They trust no one, never revealing their true plan until it's too late to thwart them. The hero chose compassion, both for themselves and others. They never give up hope, even when the challenge seems insurmountable. They know they can't do it alone and must team up for the greater good. This doesn't mean that the hero doesn't wrestle with their past. It's just that they decided not to take it out on the people around them.

As the hero of your own story, you've made choices too. You've trusted people, even forgiven them when they wronged you. You've failed at some things and spent long days and nights worrying about how to carry on. You've taken risks, despite not seeing the road ahead. Some of those risks have meant facing criticism from friends and family. You've persevered but have often felt alone on the journey thus far. Instead of turning to the dark side, you're seeking connection, ideally from people who know what you're going through. The encouraging news is that the critical missing piece to reaching your next level is simpler and more approachable than you think. I'm talking about the power of the mastermind (but not the Hans Gruber type).

Napoleon Hill describes a mastermind as the "coordination of knowledge and effort, in a spirit of harmony, between two or more people for the attainment of a definite purpose." In this time of great unknowns, we could all use allies. The obvious obstacle is finding them and getting on the same page despite being strangers. First, it is vital to note the difference between a networking event and a mastermind. When I started working in retirement planning, I didn't know anyone in my local area that fit the target market. The advice I read at the time stated that networking was the go-to strategy. I could meet new clients and get referrals if I just attended enough of these events. In theory, this was great advice. Just show up, shake hands, exchange business cards, and wait for the clients to come pouring in. Except it was much trickier than I'd hoped. These events were at all times of the day and night, and there was no telling how many people would show up. The goal was to work the room and not spend too much time talking to the same person. Even if you resonated with someone, unless you could refer to each others' business, there wasn't an incentive to stay in contact.

After seeing how most networking events were mediocre, three of us from our office got together to find a better way of meeting new people. We decided to run our own lunch-and-learn that would appeal to busy professionals. Unfortunately, we didn't have money for food, so we found companies willing to bring lunch in exchange for a captive audience. The presenters ranged from estate planners to title companies to commercial real estate developers. Our attendees were from all fields of work. Some were self-employed, like real estate agents, and others were w-2 account executives. The time of day really worked because it didn't require them to sacrifice their evenings or weekends to attend. We always started on time, kept the atmosphere casual, played music, and even ended on time. Not only did people show up every week, but they brought their colleagues. It became so popular that we hosted it twice a week. As a result, my network grew, and I saved a lot of money on lunch!

While I learned many great lessons from running these events, they weren't masterminds. In fact, I had no idea what one was. The term has become a buzzword in the last few years, but back then, it was still quite the secret of success. Had I been aware, I would have parlayed the power of those interactions into organized action. I'm okay with not knowing what I didn't know at the time because that persistence led to me finding Napoleon Hill's work. It also clarified what the role of a mastermind was in my development. Masterminds can be the critical bedrock of a business, especially for new entrepreneurs. Anyone who has left the daily corporate hustle knows the shock of self-employment. Solopreneurs lack the structure and human interaction of the typical work environment. Left to our own devices, most will drift, losing momentum or overemphasizing trivial matters that don't generate revenue. You don't need to be an entrepreneur to be part of a mastermind. Any lifelong learner who appreciates the benefit of harmonizing brainpower and effort will find tremendous value.

Technology has made masterminds easier to attend more than ever. Many are virtual or hybrid and range in focus, from business to fitness, to relationships. There's no obligation to stay with a group forever, but you should make a solid time commitment. You can even join multiple groups. The essential thing is to find groups that work best for you and to show up prepared. You should be ready to offer feedback to group members sharing their struggles and seek help when it's your turn to share. Attendees get what they put in. If someone tries to wing it or avoids deep-diving into their situation, they waste their own time and that of the group. Everyone should be a collaborator, both in encouraging members during challenging situations as well as in celebrating their wins. You aren't a teammate if you're not clapping for your teammates.

Along those same lines, if you can't find a mastermind, then start one. Write down ten people whom you'd want to meet up with on a regular basis. Contact all of them today. Tell them that it's time to level up. Don't be surprised if nine of them stare at you like you just asked them to guard your seventh Horcrux. Fortunately, it only takes one other person to start. More will follow. You don't need to know who or when. You aren't there to coach people or be their therapist. Your role is to be consistent. Leave space to be pleasantly surprised by who shows up.

Whether you join one or create one, there will be difficulties adjusting to the way masterminds operate. Working within a tight-knit group necessitates not only shared values but also shared dialect. You've worked hard to organize your plan and take action. To harness the diverse power of the group, you now must organize their collective knowledge. That means taking inventory of their specialized knowledge and learning how to support each other best. Ideas are malleable. They take shape as the energy of the group accelerates. Therefore, it's crucial to understand how to give feedback so that the person in front of you is receptive to internalizing it. Not only does it build trust, but it also clears the air for creativity to thrive.

A mastermind is only limited by the imagination and commitment of its members. It can provide insightful feedback regardless of your current level of success. It reduces frustration and shame because people like you have either been where you are or are going through it too. It is a confidential space to challenge your limiting beliefs and find camaraderie. Communication isn't limited to just the scheduled meetings. Those connections can be strengthened with accountability check-ins or just being an ear to listen to a fellow member vent. Sometimes that's all people need. Once everyone clicks, it's as if the best ideas just seem to flow, and nothing can stop you. Scaling your endeavor goes from a dream to an inevitability. Are you ready to step into your power? Villains need not apply.

FRANKIE FEGURGUR

About Frankie Fegurgur: Frankie's "burning desire" is helping people retire with dignity. Frankie distills the lessons he has learned over the last 15 years and empowers our youth to make better financial decisions than the generation before them. This is a deeply personal mission for him—he was born to high-school-aged parents, and money was always a struggle. Frankie learned that hard work, alone, wasn't the key to financial freedom and sought a more fulfilling path. Now, he serves as the COO of a nonprofit financial association based in the San Francisco Bay Area, teaching money mindfulness. He, his wife, and their two children can be found exploring, volunteering, and building throughout their community.

Author's website: *www.FrankMoneyTalk.com*
Book Series Website & Author's Bio: *www.The13StepsToRiches.com*

Fred Moskowitz

HARNESSING THE POWER OF THE PEOPLE AROUND YOU

What is a Mastermind? In his book *Think And Grow Rich*, Napoleon Hill clearly defines a Mastermind as the "Coordination of knowledge and effort, in a spirit of harmony, between two or more people, for the attainment of a definite purpose."

A Mastermind can take several forms. It may be organized as a formally structured group that meets on a defined schedule, or it can be loosely formed by your initiative based on strategic relationships with people who make up your "Board Of Advisors." In the business world, it is customary for publicly traded companies to establish a Board Of Directors, and there is absolutely no reason that you should not do the same for yourself and for your business.

Structured Mastermind Groups

In my experience of having participated in many different mastermind groups, I have found them to be highly effective. An immense power can be harnessed when you are in the presence of other like-minded individuals. And the best part? You can both give and receive on an ongoing basis, as needed. It is the perfect model of fair exchange.

When you surround yourself with the right group of people, you will greatly benefit from the counsel, support, and cooperation of the other members of the group. Everyone participates freely in the meetings, actively giving and receiving these benefits. As a result, relationships get formed between the members. There is a fair exchange of effort and energy, without expectation of anything in return other than the reciprocal support that is then given back to the group at large.

Below are the main benefits of a structured mastermind group:
- The opportunity to receive honest and objective feedback. Remember that feedback is simply information. Listen openly, take it in, see if it resonates, and allow it to influence your next steps.
- The sharing of fresh perspectives. In particular, this often may come from other members that are in a different industry than yours.
- Accountability. Members will hold each other accountable. There is something about putting your goals out there in public and then knowing that others will be watching, encouraging, and supporting you to succeed.

Brainstorming. Bringing new energy to people's ideas.

Everyone benefits from others asking questions and receiving counsel. When a question is asked by someone else, you learn from listening to their question and then hearing the answer given to them. There is tremendous learning and growth which happens simply from being present in this environment.

A mastermind does not need to have a leader. Instead, there can be a facilitator, and then the group collectively leads itself. I have found that more problems can be solved as a group than a person could solve alone.

When you join or attend a mastermind session, one of my favorite ways to make it productive for everyone is to ask some very powerful questions. Here are some sample questions that you can ask others:

- What was your latest success or achievement since the last time we met? What did you take action on from our previous meeting?
- What is your biggest challenge or obstacle that is standing in your way right now?
- What is the one thing that could solve a challenge for you right now or advance your progress forward?

Best practices when attending structured Mastermind meetings:

- Be Prepared – Show up to the meeting prepared with the question or problem that you are seeking counsel for. State your request in a brief, clear, and concise manner, and allow the group to ask any clarifying questions as needed. Providing lots of history and background stories is not helpful. It will usually confuse or distract people to the point that they get lost and are no longer sure what you are seeking. Instead, get right to the point and begin your question by stating, "My question is..."
- Referrals and introductions – If you are providing a referral or introduction to another person or business, stop, take a moment and do it right away. Immediately make the introduction with a group text message, phone call, or email introduction, which is sent out promptly. Immediate action builds momentum!
- As a recipient of counsel – At the next session, be prepared to report back to the group on what action you have taken, with an update on how the advice given previously has helped or did not work as you had anticipated. When someone provides advice or counsel, there is no greater reward than learning how the recipient took action to implement the gift that was given to them and achieved results!
- Relevance - Make sure that you and the group are a good fit for each other before you join an existing mastermind. Attend a meeting before you commit so that you can get a feel for the dynamics of the group. When you see that screening criteria are being applied,

this is usually a good sign. People may be evaluated based on a number of factors, such as your industry type, the number of years of experience, the size of your business in revenue, or your annual income or net worth. Some mastermind groups allow members by referral only, where an existing member will nominate or sponsor the newcomer.

The ancient Greek philosopher Aristotle left us with the idea that "The whole is greater than the sum of its parts." And this is exactly what you will experience in the Mastermind. The relationships and associations you create will help form your "Board Of Advisors."

Remember that people who join a Mastermind group are there to uplift, uplevel, and are genuinely interested in learning from everyone.

The Powerful Influence Of The People Around You

> *"It's better to hang out with people better than you. Pick out associates whose behavior is better than yours, and you'll drift in that direction."*
> *~ Warren Buffett*

This quote from Warren Buffett sends a very powerful message. Let's explore this further in the context of the people that are influencing you on a constant basis. The reality is this: the people around you will impact you on so many levels, consciously, subconsciously, spiritually, and energetically. And do you know who gets to decide who those people are? You do! And it is one of the most important decisions that you will be making on a constant basis.

Have you ever stopped to look at the friends and people you spend the most time with? Who are the people that you prioritize spending time together? Take a few moments to think about this right now. Next, take a piece of paper, and write down their names. It is a very worthwhile exercise and helps you better understand those relationships.

Here are some questions to think about and consider:

- When you are with your friends/colleagues, do you show up in life in a positive way? Or do you find that the worst of you tends to come out?
- Are you spending time around people who talk negatively about others or have a negative outlook on life?

When you spend a lot of time with people, what begins to happen over time is that:

- You will talk like they talk
- You will read what they read and listen to what they listen to
- You will dress as they dress
- You will act as they act
- You will eat the way they eat
- You will show up in life similar to the way they do

Do you know someone that does not seem to have any good success in life? Take a moment and think of them right now. They could be a person who experiences constant problems, financial troubles, family/relationship troubles, patterns of making poor life decisions, and generally not having a positive outlook on life. Now, take a closer look at the people they spend the most time with. Do you notice any patterns?

Take action and organize your Mastermind

If you want to improve your life, start to put yourself around people that are at the level where you would like to be. In doing this, you will see a massive shift that has many ripple effects: the conversations that are happening, the mindsets that you are exposed to, the concepts and ideas that are exchanged, and the kinds of problems that are to be solved. All these will change dramatically when you put yourself into a different environment. And there is always something to be learned from being around more experienced people. These are people that will influence you, that will lead you, and will inspire you.

They will shine a spotlight on your limiting beliefs so that you become aware of them. They will see the greatness within you and will not hesitate to call you out for playing small. They will also be there to celebrate your wins with you.

And if you find that you are the smartest person in the room, it may be time to seek out a new room.

FRED MOSKOWITZ

About Fred Moskowitz: Fred Moskowitz is a best-selling author, investment fund manager, and speaker who is on a personal mission to teach people about the power of investing in alternative asset classes, such as real estate and mortgage notes, showing them the way to diversify their capital into investments that are uncorrelated from Wall Street and the stock markets.

Through his body of work, he is teaching investors the strategies to build passive income and cash flow streams designed to flow into their bank accounts. He's a frequent event speaker and contributor to investment podcasts.

Fred is the author of *The Little Green Book of Note Investing: A Practical Guide for Getting Started with Investing in Mortgage Notes* and contributing author in *1Habit To Thrive in a Post-Covid World*.

Author's Website: *www.FredMoskowitz.com*
Book Series Website & Author's Bio: *www.The13StepsToRiches.com*

Gina Bacalski

MY FIRST TIME

I LOVE PEOPLE! I need people. I'm a Queen. I need other queens and kings. So do you. Queens and Kings need communities.

In Levi McPhearson's 3 Levels of Influence Triangle, there are three levels, as the name implies. Base level—Transactional Influence, the middle level—Reciprocal Influence, and the top level—Perpetual Influence. The higher the level of influence, the higher up the triangle you climb. The goal of the triangle is to finally get to the interaction and influence level at the top. But to do that, we've got to start somewhere.

Transaction Influence, the triangle's base, is a great place to do so. This level of interaction is one-to-one. This is what you get with most networking groups. It's a "card swap" type of interaction. The best way I can make this work and work up to higher levels of influence is with The Gina B Connect Method. Obviously, this might not work for everyone you meet, so "read the room" as you proceed. Still, for most people, this formula works with abundant success. The steps are as follows:

- Go to networking groups. When I want to grow my circle, I try to go to at least three to five a week.
- Once there, meet as many people as possible and gather their business cards, digitally or the old school, actual paper card. I like paper better because you can't "click" it away.

- Contact all of them individually. Just a brief text message and ask them to meet up for coffee. Remember, "Coffee" is an event, not a beverage.
  - ◊ VERY IMPORTANT SIDE NOTE: Keep your phone in your bag or pocket. The second you pull out your phone, you send the unsaid message that the person you are meeting with is just not that important. Even if you put the phone face down on the table next to you, this is still telling the other person that if something better or more important comes up, it takes precedence over them. I don't care if you are expecting a call from the King or the President of the United States, your momma better be dying, or your kid better be in the hospital before you take that phone out of your bag.
- When you meet them at coffee or lunch (and here is the most important part), DON'T TALK. Just listen. Don't say anything about yourself; just listen to their needs and ask engaging questions. What do they find most challenging in their business? How did they get started? What is one thing they've learned that has had the biggest influence on their decisions moving forward? This is where I envy introverts. Because fighting the urge to NOT talk about oneself is the hardest exercise of self-discipline an extrovert who loves to talk can go through.
- Then at the end of the conversation, after you let them tell all they can and want to about themselves, they will ask about you most of the time. Then and only then do you tell them what you do and how you hope to collaborate in the future.
- NOW, pull out your phone, and right then and there, connect with them on whichever social media platform they use most. Facebook, Instagram, LinkedIn, Twitter, Snapchat, Friend Face, whichever it is, find them and add them and wait till they've accepted you.
- Take a selfie with them. Make sure they look fabulous.

- Say goodbye and wish them an amazing rest of the day.
- After they've left and you're alone once more, post the photo on the social media platforms of yours and their choice and give them a shout-out. Now I give a shout-out, but until I know they are actually great at Underwater Basket Weaving, or whatever they do, I don't endorse them. Here's why: I don't know them well enough to endorse them. They've never made ME an underwater basket. They could be a nice person but a bad underwater basket weaver. So, I'll usually say something like, "Had a great coffee date with Jane Doe. She does Underwater Basket Weaving! I loved connecting with her about our mutual love for BTS and learning about her cute cat, Suga Paws." That's all you need. Keep it simple; keep it real.

Back to The 3 Levels of Influence Triangle. As we climb up, we are next at Reciprocal Influence. This is one-to-many. This is where I would try to do a joint venture with someone.

An example of this would be as a realtor if I did a joint venture with Home Organizer Jenna. She was hosting an organizers workshop (something I know would bring value to my clients who are moving or have just moved), and I would invite everyone I know to her workshop. I would help market and promote it, bringing value to Home Organizer Jenna. If any of the people that came from my efforts signed up with her, she would give me 10% of the profits she made from the people I brought to her event, which would bring value to me.

This is also a great way to meet other people in Jenna's network that I might not have yet had the opportunity to meet. Joint ventures can be a lot of fun and a great way to quickly build databases.

Climbing further up the triangle, we are now in Perpetual Influence. The top and final level! In this level of influence, your Rolodex (or network) is now my Rolodex. Before I let people in this level of influence, I need to trust this person a great deal. This amount of trust can only be reached with three things: time, repeated common experience, and common affinity. This is why going to networking and mastermind groups regularly is important.

This is also why having and building a community is so important. I started my writing group in 2017, and we've met two times a month, every month, since then. During that time, almost all of the members in my writing group have moved and bought and sold houses. Who do you think they used as their realtor? That's right, me. Who do you think they tell everyone else they know who is moving to use as their realtor? Yep, me again.

Masterminds are like networking groups on steroids! I don't know of a way to get to the top of Levi McPhearson's Triangle faster than with a mastermind group. I will never forget my first true mastermind session. One day in 2018, almost accidentally, I waltzed into a group called Amplified Minds led by Jon Kovach Jr.

The energy was amazing, the speakers were fantastic and have since become my new mentors and friends, and we played games! This "play to connect" method made me feel a kinship with others in my group who were total strangers. And then the magic happened.

We sat around a table, and Levi McPhearson's Profit Channels appeared on the screen.

People

Resources

Opportunities

Finances

Information

Technology

We were told to look at the list, pick one of those things we needed in our business, and then ask our group their ideas to help us with the Profit Channel we've chosen. Then, after we heard the person's ask, we were to go through our phones right then and there and connect them with a three-way text message with the person that we knew could help the person's ask, when applicable.

A gentleman in my group identified he needed more information about a certain part of his company that he wanted to expand. We told him of books to read and podcasts to listen to, and a few people connected him with other individuals who could provide him with the direct information he needed.

The next person to go was a woman who needed help financing her project. There were people in that very room that could help her, and she set appointments with them for a later date.

I needed information and help with systems and workflows to be more productive in my new field. I was asked clarifying questions, and the help I received was tailored specifically to my exact problems and concerns.

Each person in the group gave their ask, and we solved many problems that day. Ideas I had never thought about before suddenly burst into my mind as we talked together. The very brilliance of the "third mind" that Napolean Hill introduced was alive and firing!

My mind was absolutely blown. I didn't know the name of it at the time, but I had just experienced my very first mastermind. I knew this was where the magic happened, real change was being made, and real business was happening. I couldn't wait for the next one!

I made amazing connections with like-minded people as I went back each month. I met people in that room who have changed my and my husband's lives. That's where we met Mark Steiner, one of the smartest financial minds I've ever encountered. His company, the Latent Wealth Group, was amazing; my husband left his corporate job and joined the Latent Wealth Groups ranks. Now they are changing the world, bringing middle-class America financial techniques previously only enjoyed by the super-wealthy. I am thrilled to be joining them as the Executive Director of the Latent Wealth Real Estate Group later this month!

It was also in the group that I met Levi McPhearson and was introduced to his Prosperity Gym. In Prosperity Gym, I learned about The Buyer Code, Freedom Exercises, and the Laws of Prosperity. This alone helped reshape my life and let me release limiting beliefs and replace them with empowerment and new outlooks on life I never thought possible. My relationship with Levi has exponentially improved my life in more ways than merely financially. I appreciate my relationship with him; to this day, we are still collaborating and bringing value to high-level businessmen and women around the globe.

The point of all this is to find a group, connect, and build a tribe. People need people to make the third-mind magic happen. More minds really create the solutions we could never come up with on our own. So what will your mastermind bring to you?

GINA BACALSKI

About Gina Bacalski: Gina is a Real Estate Agent, licensed since June 2018. Her background is in Early Childhood Education where she received her Child Development Associate from the state of Utah and has an AS from BYU-Idaho. For the past 17 years, Gina thoroughly enjoyed her experience in the service industry helping families in the gifted community.

In 2019, Gina helped Jon Kovach Jr. launch Champion Circle and is now CEO of the organization. She brings her genuine love for people, high attention to detail, and strives to exceed client's expectations to the Real Estate industry and to Champion Circle.

Gina married the man of her dreams, Jay Bacalski, in San Diego, in 2013. The Bacalski's love entertaining friends and family, going on hikes, and attending movies and plays. When Gina isn't helping her clients navigate the real estate world, she will most often be found dancing and listening to BTS, watching KDramas and writing fantasy, sci-fi and romance novels.

Author's Website: *www.MyChampionCircle.com/Gina-Bacalski*
Book Series Website & Author's Bio: *www.The13StepsToRiches.com*

Griselda Beck

EXPAND YOUR MIND, ACCELERATE YOUR RESULTS!

Mastermind. Collective brain power. A think tank, community or group made up of multiple powerful leaders whose sum of wisdom, experience and expertise collectively outperform that of any individual in the group. These groups serve to expand your creativity, cut your learning curve and accelerate your results.

When we want to breakthrough to new levels in our life, family, business, career and relationships, we must surround ourselves with people who are already at or ahead of where we want to be. When we keep our environment the same, we stay the same. A mastermind can be a meeting or group, but if thought of on a macro level, it can be seen as community.

If you wish to deepen your faith, immerse yourself in a community of that faith. If you wish to make x (six, seven or eight figures), surround yourself with people who are making x figures. If you desire to be committed in your relationship, surround yourself with people who are in committed relationships. Like attracts like. You will also observe, learn and take on the habits that create the results you are looking for in your life.

We MUST be willing to be UNcomfortable for change. It only feels uncomfortable when we are not used to it yet, and when we are surrounded by those who still have our old habits while we are pushing to change.... that discomfort becomes almost unbearable and we relapse back to our comfort zone. We cannot grow in our comfort zone.

Oftentimes, people are resistant to change and feel "stuck" because they do not want to change. They want a different result, but do not want to change their habits, their environment, or their friends. What we get to create is a paradigm shift. A change in perspective, which requires a clear vision, conviction "your why" and commitment to that vision. 3 C's of vision required for change: CLARITY, CONVICTION and COMMITMENT.

Surrounding yourself with people that are on the same journey (or better yet, way ahead of you) supports you in making the small changes needed to create the results you desire. It supports you in not feeling like you're having to go at it alone. It is a bit like committing to a new way of eating that supports your health goals. When surrounded by friends that eat crappy and drink heavily, making this change can feel like torture. When surrounded by fit, healthy people, your dietary changes can feel very doable and even easy! They pick places with healthy options, they meal prep together, exchange recipes, etc. It is so much harder when you're picking healthy choices amongst a group that is eating all of your old favorite things!

Clarity of vision sounds obvious and cliche. However, we can get lost in our vision as we lean into creating it. Sometimes we lose focus, or our manifestation begins taking shape in a way we never imagined, and thus need to recalibrate. Having a sounding board for this can be incredibly supportive…especially when you "feel" lost and uninspired or stuck. Having others listen through fresh perspectives allows you to "hear" your thoughts in a new way. Others may also see things where you were too close to the detail and/or share other new possibilities they see. Sometimes just talking it out loud can support in getting clarity vs allowing the thoughts to swirl around in your head.

Mastermind groups are phenomenal tools for problem solving, strategizing, big picture thinking and innovation. Leveraging the collective wisdom of the group to bring forth new ideas and expertise is vital to cutting the learning curve.

Personally, I have found masterminds especially supportive in the following situations:

As the President of a nonprofit organization and having come from corporate, which was very much all about the profit, I found it super helpful to join a local mastermind group of professional women. In this group, I learned so much about fundraising, networked with other companies where we formed partnerships for events and collaborations to support our communities. I also was referred to several donors that supported our organization. The ideas that came from many of the participants to create events and awareness within the community for our nonprofit were things I hadn't thought of before.

As an executive leading a multi-million dollar division of a public company, I regularly participated in "think tanks" with other leaders in our industry to create policy, collaborate in philanthropy and partner to solve issues that our industry was facing in order to support consumers with quality, safety and integrity of the products available in the market. We also held internal "brainstorm" sessions with my teams as a continuous improvement and innovation initiatives. We held cross-functional sessions with key stakeholders (indirect, direct, internal and external to the company) to support in navigating the future strategy of market penetration/expansion, IP protection and company growth goals.

As an entrepreneur and CEO of my own coaching, speaking and events company I actively participate in masterminds to keep myself abreast of best business and marketing practices, networking, community building and support. As a CEO of a young small business, I don't have VPs of various departments…at the moment, that would be me and my virtual assistants. These communities have become extra special and supportive as I am able to leverage others' expertise, past experiences and support others just the same. We brainstorm together—usually each being on the hot seat for an allotted amount of time while everyone around the table supports with feedback, referrals or possible solutions/opportunities to a problem/topic being presented. In less than 15 minutes, I can usually walk away with more clarity than I would have had by mulling over an issue for weeks on my own! Entrepreneurship can be a lonely road, especially in the early years—socially and professionally. Having business besties that ride the wave of ups and downs and hold you in your highest capability even when you are feeling at your lowest is invaluable.

Likewise, there are HIGH level masterminds I join that give me the opportunity to be in a room that is "way out of my league". These usually come with a pretty price tag and are worth every penny! Why? Being surrounded by entrepreneurs that are 10 steps ahead of you supports with seeing what is possible, inspires you to keep going and THINK BIGGER! It pushes me beyond my limits, which supports me in breaking through to new levels. The wisdom and experience in these rooms is unbelievable and yet, I know I BELONG. You become an energetic match for that level of success when you surround yourself with that level of thinking and BEing. You get to witness and experience firsthand the personal habits and behind-the-scenes playbooks of leaders and companies that are already performing at the level you have envisioned for yourself and your company. The energy that buzzes through you, the clarity of ideas and vision you walk away with are exhilarating!

Bottom line, you don't have to go at it alone. Surround yourself with like minded people on the same journey. Put yourself in rooms that are "out of your league" and know that you belong. Collaborate to problem solve, strategize, and be a contribution to others and your community.

The power of the mastermind is to be served and be of service, be seen and to see, love and be loved. If what you feel you need isn't already in existence…CREATE IT!

GRISELDA BECK

About Griselda Beck: Griselda Beck, M.B.A. is a powerhouse motivational speaker and coach who combines her executive expertise with transformational leadership, mindset, life coaching, and heart-centered divine feminine energy principles. Griselda empowers women across the globe to step into their power, authenticity, hearts, and sensuality, to create incredible success in their business and freedom in their lives. She creates confident CEOs.

Griselda's clients have experienced success in quitting their 9-5 jobs, tripling their rates, getting their first client, launching their first product, and growing their business in a way that allows them to live the lifestyle and freedom they want. She has been featured as a top expert on FOX, ABC, NBC, CBS, MarketWatch, Telemundo, and named on the Top 10 Business Coaches list by Disrupt Magazine.

Griselda is an executive with over 15 years of corporate experience, founder of Latina Boss Coach and Beck Consulting Group, and serves as president for the nonprofit organization MANA de North County San Diego. She also volunteers her time teaching empowerment mindset at her local homeless shelter, Operation Hope-North County.

Author's Website: *www.LatinaBossCoach.com*
Book Series Website & Author's Bio: *www.The13StepsToRiches.com*

Jason Curtis

KNOWLEDGE, EFFORT, & OPPORTUNITY

"NO GREAT MAN EVER COMPLAINS OF WANT OF OPPORTUNITY!"
~Ralph Waldo Emerson

"THE 'MASTER MIND' MAY BE DEFIND AS: COORDINATION OF KNOWLEDGE AND EFFORT, IN A SPIRIT OF HARMONY, BETWEEN TWO OR MORE PEOPLE, FOR THE ATTAINMENT OF A DEFINITE PURPOSE."
~Napoleon Hill, Think And Grow Rich

"NO INDIVIDUAL MAY HAVE GREAT POWER WITHOUT AVAILING HIMSELF OF THE 'MASTER MIND.'"
~Napoleon Hill, Think And Grow Rich

JASON CURTIS

About Jason Curits: Jason has been a serial entrepreneur for 15 years and has enjoyed serving and helping his fellow entrepreneurs build their businesses and win in this game of life—on purpose! Jason created On Purpose Coaching because he knew, through his life experiences, that he could create an impact in others. He focuses on helping his clients create better relationships with their customers. This fosters trust and rapport while generating customer loyalty.

Jason is a Navy veteran of six years. He has sailed the seas and oceans in serving his God and country. Curtis and his wife, Brianna, have been married for eight years, and they have two children.

Author's Website: *www.JasonLaneCurtis.com*
Book Series Website & Author's Bio: *www.The13StepsToRiches.com*

Jeffrey Levine

TRUE POWER OF THE MASTERMIND

When I was eight, my father recommended that I join the biddy basketball league at the JCC. I wasn't sure that I wanted to do it since I had never played organized sports; I always liked doing things on my own. However, I agreed and was put on the worst team because I registered late.

In the first game, I couldn't make a basket, and our team lost by 30 points. Immediately after the game, the coaches spoke to the team and told everyone we were going to learn how to play defense, and the offense would take care of itself. Also, he said we had a star in Jeff Levine, and the whole team would help me score points. Even though I didn't play well that first game, the coaches said I was great in practice and would get much better. Since we were in last place, we had nothing to lose by utilizing those new strategies.

The next game was against the number one team. For some reason, I wanted to play well for the coaches and the team. Unexpectedly, we won. With 20 seconds left in the game, we had the ball and called a timeout. The coaches wanted me to take the last shot. We set up a play where I would get the ball with just a few seconds to play. Knowing I had to hurry before time expired, I shot the ball, and it went in with one second to play.

Again, the coaches spoke to us after the game. They said since we had beaten the best team, we could beat every team in the league. Game after game, we won until we entered the league championship game. Again, we were tied with the number one team with a minute to go. The coaches called the time out and said that since the other team expected me to shoot, I should fake a shot and pass it to a teammate near the basket. It worked perfectly because they had three people guarding me and no one guarding the player near the basket. He made the shot, and we won the championship.

When I was 13, I started my first year of Babe Ruth baseball. Since we were on an extended family vacation when the league started, I again ended up on the worst team in the league. Even though we didn't have the best team, we had great coaches. Our four coaches were very experienced and provided a great mastermind, enabling us to win a lot of games. Even though we weren't the best team, we had the best results. We shocked everyone in the league by winning the championship.

In my tax and financial planning practice, I had a number of mastermind members. I quickly realized that I couldn't solve all my clients' problems by myself, so I set up a mastermind of tax attorneys, accountants, insurance agents, and a banker. When I wasn't sure what to do to help with my clients' situations, I would make a quick call to one or more of my mastermind group members. Because I seemed to have a blind spot with too many of my clients' financial situations, my mastermind group always saw things I didn't.

Throughout my life, I found that the concept of the mastermind group was so important to life and business issues that I eventually co-founded an international mastermind group. It was called The Carnegie Principle. We would meet every Wednesday by Zoom and in person twice a year before the pandemic. As part of our Wednesday call, we would do some teaching and help the participants with life and business issues. What I liked most every week was that the group would help me with challenging life and business issues. Since I was a single practitioner, I often got help with business issues that I couldn't solve. Having experts on the call helped me find answers that were better than my own solutions.

After selling my business and moving to Arizona, I formed another mastermind group. This one was mainly for personal issues. Many of the people in the group were semi- or fully retired, and we were challenged to fill our time with purposeful activities. For example, I moved to Phoenix and didn't know anyone except my son. Because of that, I didn't have any friends and had a tough time socially. Even though I played in golf and tennis leagues, things didn't change, and I leaned on my new mastermind group. Many of us were facing the same challenges, and the group was extremely helpful. We met every Sunday morning for two hours. During those two hours, they made very good suggestions to me. They suggested I join the local Rotary and Chamber of Commerce, which really helped.

The best suggestion from the Sunday mastermind group was to invite people to breakfast or lunch from the Chamber or Rotary. Because of their advice, I was able to make some new friends and find other like-minded people. The mastermind group also helped me identify purposeful activities I might consider. Many of the suggestions were great and made my transition to retirement much easier. I looked forward to every Sunday morning call, and the suggestions greatly helped.

The concept of a mastermind isn't new. Henry Ford whipped poverty, illiteracy, and ignorance by aligning himself with great minds. By associating with Edison, Firestone, and others, Mr. Ford added to his brain power.

Andrew Carnegie's mastermind group consisted of a staff of approximately 50 men with whom he surrounded himself for the definite purpose of manufacturing and marketing steel. He attributed his entire fortune to the power he accumulated through his mastermind group.

You can do the same thing that many others have done, including these great leaders. Remember, if others can harness the power of a mastermind group, so can you. Maybe start with a few members and let it expand. It is worth its weight in gold.

JEFFREY LEVINE

About Jeffrey Levine: Jeffrey is a highly skilled tax planner and business strategist, as well as a published author and sought-after speaker. He's been featured in national magazines, on the cover of *Influential People Magazine*, and is a frequent featured expert on radio, talk shows, and documentaries. Jeffrey attended the prestigious Albany Academy for high school and then went on to University of Hartford at Connecticut, University of Mississippi Law School, Boston University School of Law, and earned an L.L.M. in taxation. His accolades include features in *Kiplinger and Family Circle Magazine*, as well as a dedicated commentator for Channel 6 and 13 news shows, a contributor for the *Albany Business Review*, and an announcer for WGY Radio.

Jeffrey has accumulated more than 30 years of experience as a tax attorney and certified financial planner and has given in excess of 500 speeches nationally. Levine is the executive producer and cast member in the documentary *Beyond the Secret: The Awakening*.

Levine's most current work, *Consistent Profitable Growth Map*, is a step-by-step workbook outlining easy-to-follow steps to convert consistent revenue growth to any business platform.

Author's Website: *www.JeffreyLevine.Solutions*
Book Series Website & Author's Bio: *www.The13StepsToRiches.com*

Lacey & Adam Platt

SURROUND YOURSELF WITH AMAZING PEOPLE & MY FIRST MASTERMIND

Surround Yourself With Amazing People

You've probably heard that you become who you hang around. If you hang around negative people, you will be a negative person; if you hang around poor people and take their advice, you will more than likely be poor like them. On the other hand, if you hang around positive people, you will become more positive; successful people, you'll learn to be more successful. If you hang around rich people, you will learn how to manage and make money. You get the idea. They say you become the five people you hang around the most. Why is that? It's because of influence and the power of the collective or Mastermind.

When I was younger, I got a job doing tile work, so I was always on construction sites around very tough vulgar people. Not saying everyone there was that way, but a lot of the people were, so what did I start to become? You guessed it, I started swearing more and trying to act tough and manly to fit in. I didn't really like the person I became during those few rough years. I was negative, angry, and didn't like myself. I was a reflection of those I spent a lot of my time with. Fortunately for me, I changed careers and found self-improvement to help me become more of what I am today.

I started being around people who thought positively, had goals, and talked about life differently than people on construction sites usually think of life. Life is not just to be endured, going to work every day, and having nothing to look forward to except that new episode of your favorite tv show. It's meant to be enjoyable and to learn from what struggles we do have.

It's important to find those you want to be like and start to associate and hand around people like that as much as you can. This might mean you have to get away from the toxic people in your life, maybe even family. That doesn't mean you have to cut all ties from them but limit the time you spend around those people. I've had to do this with people in my life. I have friends I don't see much of these days because we just have different perspectives of life and what we want. I still talk with them from time to time and wish them happy birthdays, but I don't hang out with them every week like I used to.

I've also been an influence on other of my friends, and they on me to keep motivating each other in our goals and dreams in life, and that is a big part of what we are talking about here.

One of the real turning points for me came when I started going to self-improvement seminars and was introduced to the mastermind concept. I started to join small mastermind groups of like- minded people like myself and wanted to achieve big things in life. This has made a huge difference in my life because the collective brain of people who want to help each other can take you further than you can by yourself. It's amazing the people you can meet. How much they can help you either connect with others who can help you, they can help brainstorm ideas to help you in your goals, or just have more experience in something that can help you and mentor you so you don't make the same mistakes they made. Mastermind groups have been a huge game-changer for me.

I've also been lucky enough to have a spouse who is on the same page as me with where we want to go in life, and that small Mastermind of just her and I is one of the most important in my life. She is one of the people I can bounce ideas off, and we talk about where we want to go in life and want to achieve. I know not everyone has a spouse like that, but it's important to find those in your life who you can use as a small mastermind and who will support you and help you and cheerleader you on towards the life you want. I also recommend finding your tribe of like-minded people who you can associate with and create or join a high-level mastermind. There can sometimes be a cost involved in those types of masterminds, but in my experience, they are worth it.

So go out, surround yourself with amazing people, and start masterminding your ideal life.

~ Adam Platt

My First Mastermind

I remember joining my first Mastermind! I can picture walking into that room as if it were yesterday! I remember thinking I was finally surrounded by my tribe, my people, the ones who think as I do, and I was super excited to start collaborating! What I didn't expect, though, was for the lady who was running the Mastermind to get up and start teaching. I remember thinking this isn't exactly what I thought a Mastermind would look like. However, over the next few months of doing this, I really grew to love the environment that was created since the group of my peers within the room seemed to elevate everyone else. This led to many inspiring conversations and some very special friendships.

Over the next few years, I had the opportunity to join several different types of Masterminds. And I did use the term "types" here very specifically. Because you will find that there are many different types of Masterminds out there.

There are the Masterminds where you have a coach stand up and teach you. These can last for several hours or even a couple days with break-out groups, self-reflection periods, and also maybe a partner exercise or two. From my experience, there is usually some kind of end goal or breakthrough you will work through either collectively or individually. The coach plans this theme or session to guide you through a preset series of events to teach you something specific.

Another type of Mastermind might begin with a game or an activity allowing you to come together as a team and create a bond within the group before you even start the Mastermind portion. This helps to "break the ice" so conversation comes more easily as you open up and share from your heart what you're working on, seeking advice and counsel, all within a safe vulnerable space.

There are more structured Masterminds where you all sit around a table and only focus on one person at a time. You listen as this person describes what they are working on, struggling with and where they need the most help. Then collectively, you throw out ideas and resources for that person and then move on and do that all over again for the next person until everyone has had a turn. This can be time-consuming but extremely helpful if you have a good group. But just a warning, it is also destructive with a bad group if unsupervised. I've experienced both.

You might also find Masterminds that are just groups of people that just come together more like a party. This is a free conversation space where you can engage in serious conversations, participate in different group experiences or activities, and/or laugh and enjoy yourself. There is no real structure, yet somehow you still walk away with action steps you want to take with your new-found friends.

I've experienced each type of these Masterminds and a few others over the years. I can tell you, in the beginning, I felt like the best one was where you just came together, bonded as a group, and then Masterminded out the plan you were working on. And I guess I still feel like this is probably the most beneficial one, timewise!

However, there are times when just coming together and almost having a party or just a group of people with the same interests enjoying one another's time and company, simply engaging in conversations is also super powerful!

Overall, in my experience with Masterminds, I would have to say there is no one "PERFECT" Mastermind. At least not that I have found up to this point. But I would say that I have had an AMAZING time enjoying all the different types of Masterminds I've had the opportunity to experience!

Go out and join a Mastermind or two and see which experience you enjoy the most. Ultimately, it's always better to be surrounded by your tribe, those people who lift you up. At the end of the day, the power of the collective mind really makes Masterminds so powerful! Enjoy!

~ Lacey Platt

LACEY & ADAM PLATT

About Lacey Platt: Lacey is an energetic, fun loving, super mom of five! She is an Achievement Coach, Speaker and new Bestselling Author who enjoys helping everyone she can by getting to know what their needs are and then loving on them in every way that she can. Her ripple effect and impact has touched the lives of so many and continues to reach more lives every single day. Allow Lacey to help you achieve your goals with proven techniques she has created and perfected over years of coaching. Lacey and her husband have built an amazing coaching business called Arise to Connect serving people all around the world.

About Adam Platt: Adam is an Achievement Coach, Speaker, Trainer, Podcast Host and now a Bestselling Author. Adam loves to help people overcome the things stopping them from having the life they really want. Adam owns and operates Arise to Connect. Adam believes that connection with yourself, others, and your higher power are the keys to achievement and greater success in life. He is impacting thousands of people's lives with his message and coaching. He lives in Utah with his wife, five daughters, and their dog, Max.

Author's Website: *www.AriseToConnect.com*
Book Series Website & Author's Bio: *www.The13StepsToRiches.com*

Louisa Jovanovich

BRINGING OUT THE BEAUTY IN YOU

This is the area of life that comes most naturally to me. I love this chapter so much. I love that I know innately and how much connecting with others is the magical way to live and create. I have been standing behind the chair for 25 years. My clients and I would have the most amazing conversations. We would say, "I wish people could hear this conversation because it really could help change lives." I have always been told people feel very safe with me and that I create a space that has them authentically share things they have never shared. In that space, it becomes so easy and effortless to share. Once the dark side of feeling alone is gone, we start feeling free. An extra burst of energy comes over us. I went from that safe space of just my client and me to creating that same space in the Mastermind. I would ask questions, and the speaker would answer. Then we open it up for others in the room to ask questions. The space of openness and safety has already been created. I know everyone participating feels safer and more confident with each question and answer.

I remember the moment someone said to me that they wished more people could hear this information. It's when my Mastermind was born. Sharing ideas and insights to discover the talent in each person and help leverage that talent to make their life more successful and meaningful. It became a safe and powerful place to connect. Life took a different turn as I discovered things about myself that I didn't know before. I saw what would bring up ideas and how people responded to them. Collecting evidence. I would hear statements like, "Louisa said." That became a regular event. I didn't know I had so many ideas until I heard that enough times. I saw that my friend Annie was amazing at organizing things and creating structure. My friend Fatima is grounded and led. She has a way of making sure you feel so seen and loved. Being a photographer and holding space for anyone in her lens to show up beautifully. Everyone's talents were coming to life. It was being highlighted and appreciated.

I am now participating in many Masterminds and hosting my own. Each one took on a life of its own, with a different vision, mission, and purpose. I am growing and learning. What I get from being a participant is very different from leading my own. I show up so differently in each one, yet each one has so much value. Stepping into a leadership role for me is now very comfortable. However, I did not know that about myself for so long. As a little girl who was never picked to be a team captain in school, I thought to be a leader, someone else had to choose you to be put in that role. Now, I know that leaders choose themselves through hard work and commitment to growth. They don't wait for permission to show up. My steps every day to becoming an expert in my field were creating the confidence I needed to choose myself and step into my power.

The opportunity to receive and give is a powerful experience. I always wanted to meditate and journal daily. I realized I could succeed at this if I could create a group, inviting people to meditate and journal with me. It would have more energy if there was an accountability group. I started it fairly easily. I would stream other people's meditations, then we would journal together. I was getting more comfortable and confident. I started doing the grounding before streaming the meditation. The experience was so great and empowering. I was really enjoying being in the flow.

The feedback was great. People wanted more of that instead of streaming the meditations. I was getting more and more comfortable. The group was a family. There were regulars showing up.

As I have shared in previous chapters, I got clarity on moving my children from Florida to LA because of this work. Thank goodness for this team because one of my Mastermind members was also in another Mastermind. She knew someone who worked for a company that could pack and move my family. This was a huge blessing for me. What could have been a very stressful experience was effortless. Creating my own tribe was so great. If my life was a puzzle, the pieces were falling into place. Things were being shown clearly, one step after another.

What does it mean to be in the flow? When things start falling into place. Life is happening in a peaceful and calm way. I am in a place of acceptance and avoiding resistance. If you don't know this about me by now, I'll tell you that I am an evidence collector. I look for what I or others do and what the results are. I try to avoid doing or removing certain things that the evidence shows don't contribute to or contaminate my life and add the things that math is clearly showing are working.

Fun stories in support of my statement above—I had a client who was unhappy in her relationship and wanted to leave her husband. She wanted to be with someone more ambitious. Her husband did not work super hard, although he went to work and came home, and everything he made he shared with his family. She found herself bored. She really wanted to be with someone who was more exciting out in the world and making lots of money with lots of charisma. Well, she walked out of her marriage. She did find herself a very successful man. He had lots of money, and she was so excited about the life she saw possible. She had been hoping for this, so she married him, only to find out that she now had an allowance. A very small amount he gave her to spend on herself. She had way more freedom and money in the previous relationship. She was following what she thought would make her happy and did not know there was work she could have done to get what she was looking for. Awareness is key to deep diving into who we are and what we really want. How many of us jump from thing to thing, thinking that the next jump will lead us to the magic we think we need? Or convincing oneself that "this" is the opportunity I have been waiting for, just to discover that we attracted exactly what we did not want. There are laws of the universe. It works in a specific manner.

These thoughts, kept to ourselves, are running the internal dialogue to what we think we need to do. I have had people in my Mastermind write everything they say they want. We have an opportunity to share it with one another. During the sharing time, it never fails that everyone is only aware of what they do not want in life. So, what are they attracting?

Yes, you got it. Everything they don't want.

Having space to get clear on our thoughts is the key. Getting clear on what we have been doing that is not working and confirmation to keep doing the things that are working. Helping each other see what may be in the blind spot. Seeing that we are not alone is a great place to start.

Then I offer one-on-one coaching to visit those thoughts and behaviors that have been running the show in our subconscious mind. To show the importance of being aware of how those thoughts got us here. They have become so part of the way we think that we don't even realize we have control over them. As people are sharing, I am listening for the core beliefs that they have created.

For example, I have a very close friend whose daughter died in a very tragic car accident. A few times, when she left me a message from the car, she would say, "I am going to get off now because I don't want to die."

Of course, we all know not to be on the phone while driving, but we do not usually use sentences as strong as "I will hang up now because I do not want to die." She has been saying this sentence since her daughter's passing and not realizing she was saying it. I am not saying that she will manifest dying on the road because of this sentence. However, I am saying there is a subconscious fear she is resisting. Being present in our subconscious fears is where the gold is.

When we bring them to our conscious minds and become aware of them, we create a new possibility that lights us up. We get excited about what we have now created and live in that new place. Once we get great at that new one, we step into another one. I will share three of mine that I have taken on that have been working for me. When I'm holding something, I say the sentence, "don't put it down; put it away." This has really helped me free up time in my day. I don't create a mess, and there is structure to my day. I feel better knowing about eliminating rework, and my life is more organized. Another is, "I become aware, and I follow through." Now things just get done easily and smoothly because of this sentence. Last but not least is, "I'm powerful beyond all measure. I am capable of being financially abundant."

I hope this has created some insight for you.

LOUISA JOVANOVICH

About Louisa Jovanovich: Louisa is the founder of Connect with Source. She is a mindfulness and emotional intelligence coach. She helps identify blindspots and create new beliefs which empower her clients to access a life they have never dreamed possible. She has completed 20 years of personal and transformational growth including Landmark Forum, Gratitude Training, and is a Clarity Catalyst Certified trainer. She works with entrepreneurs who seek clarity and want to up-level their lives.

Her life experiences and school of hard knocks are what make her a knowledgeable and compassionate leader and enable her to help guide others through the process of looking for answers within in order to find success and breakthrough their limiting beliefs. Her unique coaching techniques help her clients see the truth behind the stories that are keeping them stuck in the reality that they created.

Louisa is a single mother of two teenagers living in LA. Her love and compassion towards others are her superpowers, helping others reclaim their confidence, find their voice, and know their worth.

Author's Website: *www.ConnectWithSource.com*
Book Series Website & Author's Bio: *www.The13StepsToRiches.com*

Lynda Sunshine West

MASTER WHAT?

In 2014, I had never heard the word mastermind. It wasn't until I met someone who would soon become the greatest mentor I ever met who would teach me what a mastermind is and its power if I was willing to open my mind to the possibilities.

I have worked in the corporate world for 36 years and have had 49 jobs; my last job was as a Judicial Assistant for a Judge in the Ninth Circuit Court of Appeals. Through all of those jobs, I never felt appreciated and felt like my voice didn't matter.

When I met Dr. Greg Reid in 2015, I had no idea that my life was about to change and shift into something way bigger than I ever could have imagined.

I grew up in a volatile, abusive, alcoholic household, and it created a young girl who didn't believe in herself. Unfortunately, I carried that disbelief around for 51 years. Even though my husband of 33 years has always believed in me and told me how brilliant and amazing I am, I just couldn't seem to shake my old belief that I was stupid and ignorant and had no value on this planet.

Sometimes we need people outside of our circle who believe in us to help us tap into who we really are. My husband was too close to me for me to believe him. I always thought he was just saying that to be nice to me because "Who could honestly think that about me?"

It was November of 2014 when I decided to leave my job working for the judge to embark on a new journey called entrepreneurship. I didn't know anything about being a successful business owner, but I desired it so much that I jumped out of that job without a net and decided there was no turning back. While this was a foolish decision, because I made more money on that job than I ever did on any other job, it was necessary. Sometimes our most foolish decisions are our greatest decisions. This was a necessary move because I so desperately wanted to change my life. No one could tell me it was a bad move because I simply couldn't hear what they were saying.

Sometimes during this journey called "life," we need to do things just because we need to do them. There doesn't always have to be a reason for what we do (we don't always have to know the reason for what we do), and that's okay.

I was attending a vision board seminar when I heard Dr. Reid speak for the first time. His speech really moved me. It inspired and motivated me to take an action I wouldn't normally have taken due to fear. I didn't let my fear stop me from taking the steps necessary to get a different result in my life. The definition of insanity is doing the same thing over and over again and expecting a different result. I knew I needed to do something different to get a different result.

That one decision completely changed the trajectory of my life, and that's when I was introduced to something called "a mastermind." I started meeting new people who were successful in life and business and they, too, became mentors of mine. They taught me things I had never heard of. They helped me envision what success looks like and that I could have it. They helped me become focused on my business, so I could experience my own success. They helped me break through fears that had been stopping me from living the life I was meant to live. Through the power of the mastermind, I gained more knowledge and connections to incredible people and have been able to move into a position of knowing who I am and the value that I offer this planet.

Being surrounded by people who are successfully doing what you want and then asking for help from them to get the success that you want is one of the things that the mastermind can do for you. I spent many years afraid to ask for help because I didn't want to feel like I didn't know anything. Through masterminding, though, I found people who truly wanted to help me move to the next level in life and in business. In addition, they freely gave me the advice I needed to "grow up" in my business.

Motivational speaker Jim Rohn said, "You're the average of the five people you spend the most time with." If this is the case, and you want to grow, you need to find higher-minded people who can help you get to where you want to be. But, on the other hand, if you keep hanging out with the same people, you will continue to get the same results.

One of my favorite things about a mastermind is that everybody comes together from different walks of life with different experiences and successes. So we can tap into each other's experiences, learn from each other, and grow. If you're in a mastermind and provide all the value, then you are more of a teacher, mentor, and coach rather than part of the mastermind. Allowing everyone to share their value is where the power of the mastermind comes in.

Sometimes it can be intimidating to be surrounded by so many successful people and feel you don't have enough value to offer. I get it. I have been intimidated many times, but I keep pushing through it because I realize I can't grow if I don't hang out with them.

There was one instance when we were in a mastermind with a gentleman who was a billionaire. This was a very eye-opening experience for me.

He was extremely helpful in responding to our business questions, and I was shocked when he raised his hand and said, "I want to be in the hot seat." My first thought was, "How can I possibly provide value for this billionaire?" He hopped into the hot seat and started sharing his challenge. As he spoke, my thought shifted, "I can help in this area." His challenge had nothing to do with business. He was a billionaire. What kind of help could I give him? His challenge was personal. It was about a woman he had met recently in whom he was interested but didn't know how to ask her out. His wife had passed away many years earlier, and he didn't know how to get back into the dating game. While I had been married for almost 30 years and didn't know anything about dating, I am a woman, and I was able to give feed-forward to help him with his plight. I raised my hand and provided valuable information. He thanked me, and I realized that masterminding isn't always about helping others create more money.

Sometimes masterminding is about business, and sometimes it's personal. Still, it's always an opportunity to learn and grow and to tap into other people's minds by utilizing their experiences and how they have overcome challenges in their own lives. One thing we can realize by being in a mastermind is knowing that we are not alone and there are other people out there who want to see us succeed and help us succeed. I'm grateful for being introduced to masterminding in 2015. It has changed my life, and I will continue to mastermind until I'm no longer here.

LYNDA SUNSHINE WEST

About Lynda Sunshine West: As the Founder and CEO of Action Takers Publishing, Lynda Sunshine West's mission is to empower 5 million women and men to share their stories with the world to make a greater impact on the planet. She is affectionately known as The Queen of Collaboration. Lynda Sunshine is a Book Publisher, Speaker, Multiple Times #1 International Bestselling Author, Executive Film Producer, and a Red Carpet Interviewer. At the age of five, she ran away and was gone an entire week. She came home riddled with fears that stopped her from living. At age 51, she decided to face one fear every day for an entire year. In doing so, she gained an exorbitant amount of confidence and now uses what she learned to fulfill her mission. She believes in cooperation and collaboration and loves connecting with like-minded people.

Author's Website: *www.ActionTakersPublishing.com*
Book Series Website & Author's Bio: *www.The13StepsToRiches.com*

Maris Segal & Ken Ashby

CONVERTING ENERGY INTO WHAT MATTERS WITH MASTERMINDS

Science tells us that the universe is "pure energy" and that energy is the source of infinite intelligence, unlimited possibilities, and imagination without borders. Is this just "woo-woo," you know, that dubiously or outlandishly mystical, supernatural, and unscientific kind-of-speak? Not in the least! Research has proven that the universe is 95% energy and only 5% matter. Further, energy creates matter, and the ratio of 95/5 never changes. The human race is continuously converting energy into matter, specifically summoning our energy to create "what matters most" to us!

As business and personal leadership consultants and coaches, we often navigate a "vision" conversation with our clients and their teams around these key questions, "What do you want?" "What are you committed to bringing about in your personal and /or professional life, and by when?" "What skills and who will it take to support bringing your desires and vision into reality?" and "What matters to you right now?" This is where relationships are important! Relationships are the most significant factors impacting and influencing every aspect of our lives. Every relationship at work, home and with the planet begins first with connecting to ourselves, our energy, and our desires to make something happen. The second is connecting with someone and/or something to bring it about.

Think about it this way, if you are in "love," and that's what "matters most" to you right now, you are consistently converting your energy into an expression of that love to create a meaningful relationship, an energy exchange between you and someone else. If your business and accumulating wealth are what "matters most" to you, then your energy will be channeled in that direction. When you have a "vision that matters" and you are committed, you call upon all the forces within you to generate and manifest that vision, thereby turning your energy of thought and imagination into action to support bringing the vision that calls you to life! Can you do it alone? Why would you?

Creating something new in our lives is directly proportional to the strengths of energy we direct toward that love, wealth, and vision we truly desire with every electron, atom, and cell of our being. The notable inventor Nikola Tesla said it succinctly, "If you want to find the secrets of the universe, think in terms of energy, frequency, and vibration."

Big audacious visions in any aspect of our lives need the expertise and power of multiple minds connected and "working in harmony" to generate collective and collaborative energy that transcends one's individual mind and capabilities. It is the same with batteries; the more you link together, the more energy and power are generated. Ask Elon Musk, whose electric vehicle, the Tesla, a shout-out to Nikola for sure, links 8,256 batteries to get us to the store and back. The equivalent of linking batteries to generate power to propel a great vision is a Mastermind, many minds working in harmony, like batteries, to accomplish a shared goal.

Your Mastermind – Circles of Trust and Skills

When it comes to human relations and supporting your desires, two distinct circles of people will be paramount throughout your life. First, consider who is in your Trust Circle: the people in your life who are authentically there for you as you navigate change and growth, those whose radical honesty, feedback, wisdom, coaching, nurturing, and expertise you trust.

Most often, this includes a core of family and friends. Second, consider the skilled support your vision and plans will require in your Skills Circle: those with the professional expertise and technical knowledge you may not possess. In select cases, there may be some overlap. As you build a plan for your vision, this will answer the questions noted earlier, "What skills and who will it take to support bringing your desires and vision into reality?" This is a Mastermind, and you never want to be without one! Masterminds, at work or at home, are created from "desire." Vision is the big-picture perspective of what you believe and see as possible in the future. It's big and attainable in support of your desires. For example, doubling the size of your team and business, a family trip, running a marathon, or finding a mate. When you are committed, you can see and live it as if it has already happened. A clear, concise vision is the key to accomplishing our goals and the linchpin to enrolling the support of your Trust Circles and Skill Circles.

Putting your vision to paper solidifies your intentions and supports goal setting. "My vision is…". Writing a strong personal or professional vision statement articulates an aspiration for an imagined and attainable goal. A clear vision, when shared consistently, evokes emotion and inspires family, staff, investors, and clients to engage their resources and partner with you to bring your vision to fruition. When we get pulled off track, we tap back into the vision and call upon our Trust Circle and Skills Circle! Our intention and vision keep the Mastermind moving toward one purpose and navigating change along the way to adapt as needed.

Your Mastermind TEAM!

Most people possess a unique ability to do something unthought-of by following a dream with the aid and support of specialists. Too often, people fail to actualize a whopper of an idea because fear and ego get in the way. They do not ask for support because they are afraid to "get it wrong" or be seen as "weak." Committing to your vision means stepping through your fear and ego to choose the right **TEAM** around you! Tactically

Enrolling Acute Masterminds/**TEAM** drives collaborative relationships and, ultimately, success. Choosing the right people can be both simple and challenging at the same time. Out of all the qualified prospects with the specialized skills and knowledge required, it is important to engage the experts who align with your vision, style, and the energy flow of your existing team (if one or more individuals are already in place). At the same time, gathering a diverse group of formally trained and experientially trained individuals who will positively challenge your thinking to ensure a 360 perspective is important.

Collaborating liberates us from feeling overwhelmed when faced with a seemingly insurmountable project. Building a team with knowledge pertinent to the vision increases the probability of success. Surrounding ourselves with those trained in specific areas provides heightened confidence and empowerment. Increased optimism in the outcome brings a positive outlook for the project and becomes an affirmation for our whole being.

Once the **TEAM** principle has been used, whether on a grand or small scale, we follow these essential five steps in our creative process, utilizing our Mastermind at every turn: 1) Inspiration, 2) Visualization, 3) Creation, 4) Acknowledgement, 5) Evaluation. Skipping any of these steps can bring a great idea to a rapid demise.

Too often, the owner of a whopper of an idea jumps from step one (Inspiration) straight to step five (Evaluation) before even starting. These phrases (often only in the inspired owner's mind) come up; "Oh, this has probably been done before," "There are others who know how to do this better than me," "It's probably too expensive," "Who am I to think I can do this." Do those phrases sound familiar? The "best practice" is always to be curious and be willing to ask questions of your Mastermind. Trust their clarity.

We're often asked, "How big should my professional Mastermind be, and how often do you recommend we meet?" Depending on its purpose (networking or requesting expert counsel), Masterminds will vary in size. You may call on them regularly in a group setting (monthly) or individually. There is no right or wrong as long as all are aligned on expectations, processes, and systems. We find that groups from 6 to 20 are especially effective. Communication is key when having these sessions, and recording is also wise so that you can be present and focused on what is being shared versus taking notes.

As a personal and/or business strategy, we invite you to strategically share your time by participating in others' Masterminds as well. Not only will they benefit from your expertise, but the engagement with them will also sharpen your skills, connect you to current trends, deepen your network, and support your ongoing leadership.

Vision and planning in your personal or professional life are not lone wolf jobs. Connecting your energy and expertise with others leverages everyone's gifts to benefit all, not to mention how good it feels when all succeed together. Relationships are the inside-outside cornerstones and work best when giving, receiving, and trusting in yourself and others. We step into our leadership by creating, reviving, or reinventing relationships that will lift our "desires and our vision" to the magic point of harmonic flow.

Reflections:

What do you want?

What are you committed to bringing about in your personal and/or professional life, and by when? What skills and who will it take to support bringing your desires and vision into reality?

MARIS SEGAL & KEN ASHBY

About Maris Segal and Ken Ashby: From Mindset to Marketing, Ken Ashby & Maris Segal, a husband and wife dynamic duo, have spent the last thirty-plus years bringing an innovative, collaborative voice to issues, causes, and brands. As entrepreneurs, activists, business strategists, executive producers, coaches, authors, speakers, and trainers, Ken & Maris work with the public and private sectors from boardrooms and classrooms to the world stage. They are known for creating high touch experiences that unite diverse populations across a broad spectrum of business, policy, and social issues.

Their leadership expertise in Business Relationship Marketing, Organizational Change & Cultural Inclusion, Personal Growth, Project Management, Public Affairs, and Philanthropy Strategies has been called upon by companies and their agencies. Their experience includes: consumer and financial brands, Olympic organizers, Super Bowls, America's 400th Anniversary, Harvard Kennedy School, Archdiocese of LA and NY Papal visit planners, the White House and celebrities across the arts, entertainment, sports, and culinary genres.

With Ken's expertise as an award-winning singer-songwriter, they launched ONE SONG, a song-writing workshop series designed to unleash creativity in individuals and teams.

Their DRIVE method: **D**esire, **R**elationships, **I**ntention, **V**ision and **E**mpowerment sits at the core of their companies Prosody Creative Services, ONE SONG, and Segal Leadership Global to set a path for every client to Build High Performing Businesses & Elevate Personal & Professional Leadership for Maximum Impact & a 360-degree Thriving Life!

Author's Website: *www.ProsodyCreativeServices.com*
Book Series Website & Author's Bio: *www.The13StepsToRiches.com*

Mel Mason

MASTERMIND YOUR WAY TOWARD ANYTHING

Leaning into Co-Dependence Increases Your Ability to Succeed

In early September 2022, I completed the fourth most difficult marathon in the world. I'm still in shock because nine months before the race, I swore I would never become a runner. Never. Being a runner means shin splints, knee replacements, and tendon tears—none of which sound appealing to me. But, to my surprise, I finished the Kauai Marathon without any of these issues. As much as I'd like to say it was all me, I wouldn't have been able to complete the run without my mastermind.

Napoleon Hill states, "A Mastermind is a coordination of knowledge, effort, and a spirit of harmony between two or more people to attain a definite purpose." Essentially, it's a gathering of people with the intention of working toward a specific goal. When most people think of a mastermind, they picture a group of well-dressed elites gathered around a large conference table to discuss business opportunities. Still, a mastermind can be formed for any pursuit. For example, bringing together a group of people to aid in running a marathon, writing a book, or learning to cook are all definite purposes.

In terms of size, a mastermind can be a group of two, thirty, or one hundred people, so long as there is a defined aim. A mastermind could be a book club, a theater troupe, or a coach working with a client. Ideally, there are regular mastermind meets, but communication can be as flexible as a group chat or as structured as a scheduled weekly meeting.

Many of us become stuck in the mentality that we must do it all ourselves or our achievements don't count. Yet, no one can produce an outcome on their own. Humans, by nature, are co-dependent. Babies need care, children need raising, and teens need guidance. Even as adults, we rely on others to employ us, supply the goods we consume, and repair our cars. As Napoleon Hill said, "No mind is complete by itself. It needs contact and association with other minds to grow and expand."

Many people claim the title of "lone wolf" as a badge of honor when it is a death sentence in nature. Wolves are literally pack animals—they are meant to live in groups! An independent (lone) wolf will surely perish before the co-dependent wolves. Wolves benefit from the pack life, bearing the yoke of survival in the wilderness, sharing food, keeping warm, and protecting each other.

Similarly, people are meant to interact with each other. Apart from being inherently social creatures, individual humans cannot be expected to know everything about the world and perform every task necessary for survival. As evidence of human co-dependence, people call plumbers to fix toilets, hire coaches to help them declutter their spaces, and invoice clients so they can pay their bills.

I often work with clients who admit they identify as "lone wolves." Their cluttered homes result from thinking they can do it all by themselves. Eventually, they become so overwhelmed they reach out to me. The irony is because they have 'hired' me, they think they are maintaining their "lone wolf" status. Paying someone for help is still asking for help.

Humans are not meant to function independently. Even automobile mogul Henry Ford understood the power of interdependence and the mastermind. Ford had a basic understanding of cars and engines but didn't know how to build a vehicle for the masses. What he did know were lots of people who could fill in his knowledge gaps. He brought engineers, designers, and mechanics under one roof and from a thick Rolodex, could find all the specialized knowledge he needed to build a car manufacturing empire.

The mastermind demands co-dependence. It recognizes the strength of reaching out to others for all kinds of help. To run the Kauai Marathon, I relied on my mastermind group. My teammates and I shared a running coach, a strength training coach, and a nutrition coach. The running coach helped us with our stride, foot strike, and running form. The strength coach focused on building our muscles to prevent injury and withstand the grueling race. The nutrition coach ensured we were consuming the right balance of carbs and fats so our bodies would perform optimally. Weekly coaching calls kept everyone accountable to their mileage goals, and a group chat allowed us to problem-solve hurdles as soon as they arose. Without this mastermind, I would have struggled to amass the knowledge and experience required to complete a marathon and remain (literally) standing.

It might seem overwhelming to start a mastermind, but if broken down into smaller pieces, it's relatively easy. The first key is to define the purpose. A mastermind isn't simply a catch-up chat with a friend. There must be a focus in the meet-up for it to qualify as a mastermind. For example, if the chat with a friend is to exchange recipes for family meals, then the chat is a mastermind.

Moreover, masterminds don't have to be a formal sit-down with an agenda. They can be as lax as joining a local gardeners' Facebook group or a Tiki Bar Reddit forum. And if you can't find a friend or group to join in your definite purpose, there are many coaches, guides, and tutors available for hire.

While it might be beneficial to join an established mastermind, such as a quilting circle, recreational sports team, or business entrepreneurs' club, it is not required. In fact, sometimes, a diverse group of people in a mastermind is more helpful than a homogenous one. For example, a friend wanted feedback on a draft of a book he wrote, so he created a mastermind with various people. As a result, he now has points of view on his book from a career carpenter, a single parent, and his mom. It's not that he's going to change or cut exactly what each person suggested, but he gained a better sense of how different types of people may react to the stories and ideas in his book. He couldn't have gained those insights without a mastermind.

One common error in a mastermind's practice is failing to act on the knowledge of the mastermind. It sounds silly, but many people stall on the chatting, dreaming, and planning pieces of a mastermind and never apply what they've learned to their definite purpose. This willful dismissal of new insight is often driven by the need to be the "lone wolf," as if taking advice or trying someone else's idea means the crumbling of a person's individual spirit.

On my journey to run a marathon, I applied the mastermind insights with great success—I ran the La Jolla Half Marathon about five months into my training and felt wicked good afterwards. High on a sense of accomplishment and endorphins, I was tempted to leave the marathon and head straight to the climbing wall, but I resisted for one day. My coaches told me I would need a day of recovery for each mile run. But ten days seemed like a long time, and I felt fine! Plus, they hadn't explicitly said I couldn't work my muscles, only "no running."

I snuck off to the rock gym and did ninety minutes of climbing—I usually only do one hour. Two days later, I was back for another hour-and-a-half-long session, and I helped a decluttering client the following day. For several hours, I hauled broken furniture and clunky old housewares over the lip of a giant dumpster.

The next morning, I felt like I had been hit by a Mack Truck loaded with all the world's clutter. I felt so physically broken and exhausted I didn't think I would recover. Instead of a ten-day recovery, my lone wolfing resulted in a twenty-day healing period. The next time around, I listened to the mastermind.

If people ignore their mastermind, they are more likely to burn out as they progress toward their goals. For me, I burned out physically. If my friend working on a book refused to listen to the mastermind he created, he might have burned out after the first draft, too exhausted and entangled in his own writing to even pick up the pen to churn out a better second draft. It seems ridiculous that one would start a mastermind only to dismiss the ideas, insights, and feedback. Still, this rookie mistake is common because most people have operated for so long under the lone wolf mentality.

Caught in the lone wolf perspective, we miss out on the incredible satisfaction and joy of co-dependence in a mastermind. A mastermind helps us succeed, and the codependency baked into the mastermind enriches our life with a deeper sense of connectedness to our goals and community. Having a group of mentors and peers cheer you on toward the finish line makes completing a task that much sweeter. And when others feel they are a part of your journey, the celebration and support around you amplify. When I crossed the finish line at the Kauai Marathon, I didn't stop running when my foot crossed the checked line. Instead, I ran straight for my teammates and coaches—the whole mastermind.

MEL MASON

About Mel Mason: International best-selling author Mel Mason is The Clutter Expert, and as a sexual abuse survivor, she grew up depressed, suicidal, and surrounded by clutter. What she realized after coming back from the brink of despair and getting through her own chaos was that the outside is just a mirror of the inside, and if you only address the outside without changing the inside, the clutter keeps coming back.

That set her on a mission to empower people around the world to get free from clutter inside and out, so they can experience happiness and abundance in every area of their lives.

She is the author of Freedom from Clutter: The Guaranteed, Foolproof, Step-by-Step Process to Remove the Stuff That's Weighing You Down.

Author's website: *www.FreeGiftFromMel.com*
Book Series Website & Author's Bio: *www.The13StepsToRiches.com*

Dr. Miatta Hampton

IRON SHARPENS IRON

Being in community gives you a sense of belonging. Nothing feels better than knowing you have a tribe, a group of individuals to connect with, and people headed in the same direction. Living harmoniously in a community tied together by thoughts, beliefs, values, vision, and purpose is an ingredient to finding success in life. Being in community gives you the power to be connected to something bigger than yourself. Furthermore, community grants you support that you would not otherwise have. The old African proverb says, "If you want to go fast, go alone. If you want to go far, go together". This power is harnessed when you can come together collectively to create impact and have significance. If you want to turn your pain and purpose into profit, you will need help. You need people who believe in you and who you are becoming. There is no such thing as self-made, and if you are going to pull off your dreams and your vision, you need people. Community is a necessity. Why, you ask? Who else will assist you with planning, coordinating, executing, and promoting? I am reminded of a bible verse that says, "As iron sharpens iron, so one person sharpens another" (Proverbs 27:17).

I had gotten lost in being a wife, mother, and an employee. All my life, I either worked two jobs or worked full-time and attended college full-time. I had conditioned myself to perform multiple activities simultaneously, and for the first time in my life, I had committed to just work and family. I had been consumed with going to work, rushing to recitals, basketball games, and being a chaffer. I was fizzling out and growing frustrated. I knew there had to be more to life than just working and attending my kids' school events. I wanted something for myself. Something that would give me significance while also creating impact.

I wanted to gain clarity of my identity and be who I was called to be. I had become a human doing and not a human being. I was everything to everybody, and I was nothing to myself. I needed change, and I needed it quickly. It was like my life had flashed before my eyes, and I could see myself and my husband as empty nesters. I began to think about what I would do and who I would be once the kids were adults and no longer in our home. I had nothing to lean on. I didn't even have a hobby. I had made education my focus, and without sitting in a classroom, I had no idea what to do with my life. I was raised to believe that you get an education, get a good job, find a spouse, get married, have kids, work your job until retirement and then travel. Well, what if I wanted to travel now? What if I didn't want to wait to enjoy life? What if I wanted time and freedom now. I had no idea how to make sense of any of what I was feeling. And just like that, I found my first community on Facebook, or should I say due to the wonderful algorithm my community found me!

I had the slightest idea about business. Aside from filing for my LLC, I was lost. February 2020 would be the end and the beginning. The end of my traveling through life with the lack of clarity for my purpose and the beginning of understanding my vision and how community was one of the vehicles to get me close to living life on purpose according to my dreams. My eyes would be open to the notion that I don't have to have all the answers. I don't need to be the smartest person in the room. I don't have to do this alone. Iron sharpens iron, and there is power in connectivity and proximity. My eyes were opened to the fact that life nor business is meant to be done solo. To get to the next level, you need people. People to push you into your destiny, people to catapult you into creative spaces, people to change the trajectory of your life.

Benefits of being in a community

In a community, you will find the support you need to take massive action to take your life and business to the next level. You will share advice with high-achieving solutions-orientated individuals. You will share your success and lessons learned. You will learn to be decisive and become more organized in your thinking. Most importantly, you will learn the power of persistence and accountability. Below are four benefits of joining a community or a peer group:

Able to get feedback

Being in a community that provides feedback allows individuals to receive wisdom and recommendations geared toward relevant results. It is an environment that fosters support, encouragement, and course correction to improve performance.

Can run the beta test

Suppose you have not figured out your target audience or are looking to test your products on real people. In that case, a community is a great way to work out bugs for your products. Beta testing in a community is a great opportunity to get usability, presentation, and price point feedback.

Place to find clarity

Everyone with a business needs clarity. Clarity helps us to define our purpose, direction, and strategy. For a business to function properly, you need clarity. Having a community that you can grow with that offers insight can help you understand your strengths and weaknesses and those of the business. It can help you discover your why, understand how others see you, and what makes you different.

A place to understand your audience

Before selling anything, you need to know who you are selling to. To discover who you are selling to, you must do market research. Performing research will allow you to talk to and engage your potential audience or, at a minimum, discover if you have what people want.

To be effective in a community, you must have faith, a plan, persistence, and the power of influence. Your influence is used to equip and empower those connected to you to push the mission and vision of your dreams. It is essential that you understand the capacity and bandwidth of those that are connected to you. Iron sharpens iron. It was a great feeling being in a peer group where I could celebrate wins with no judgment and get insight and clarity. Don't be afraid to disconnect from people, places, or spaces that do not add value to you, and you don't add value to it.

Take some time and reflect on the questions below.

> Do you add value to those that you are connected to? How?
>
> Do you enhance your quality of life?
>
> Do people get better as a result of being connected to you?
>
> Who is your accountability partner?
>
> When it comes to my business, I need clarity in this area?

To book me as a speaker, email *info@drmiattaspeaks.com*
Follow me on Instagram, Facebook, and Clubhouse: *@drmiattahampton*

DR. MIATTA HAMPTON

About Dr. Miatta Hampton: Dr. Miatta Hampton is a nurse leader, #1 best-selling author, speaker, coach, and minister. Miatta impacts others with her powerful, relatable messages of pursing purpose, and she empowers her audiences to live life on purpose and according to their dreams. She coaches and inspires women to turn chaos into cozy, pivot to success, and how to profit in adversity. Miatta provides tools and resources for personal, professional, and financial growth.

Author's website: *www.DrMiattaSpeaks.com*
Book Series Website & Author's Bio: *www.The13StepsToRiches.com*

Michael D. Butler

THE MASTERMIND EVOLUTION

Masterminds have been around for thousands of years; they are not a new concept. Great global leaders, philosophers, and philanthropists throughout history have leveraged the power of the mastermind to uncover the best wisdom for daily living and practical application in multiple industries to better humanity. The power of the mastermind has been used for good and evil throughout history, but for the sake of this chapter, we'll look at only the positive impact of the mastermind, and I'll use the words mentor and mastermind member interchangeably. The concept of the mastermind has gained popularity in recent years, and more and more individuals of all ages are benefiting from the concept.

Over the years, in my own life, I have personally grown from the wisdom of Solomon and the advice of great thinkers and great achievers from multiple industries.

Utilizing the power of a mastermind began with me at an early age. Even though I didn't label it that or understand what I was doing, I was vetting my inner circle like a CEO hiring his starting lineup before going public.

My first mastermind was my mom, dad, and brother. Later they evolved into my coach, schoolteacher, and youth pastor. They later became my wife, business partner, and carefully selected inner circle of friends, attorneys, CPAs, business mentors, and even my customers.

Misconceptions about Masterminds

Mastermind members don't have to live in your same time frame.

It's helpful if your mentor is contemporary to your timeline but not required. In the internet age, it's easier to follow someone and glean from their wisdom, especially if they've left a lot of their writings behind.

Mastermind members don't have to live in the same country.

By the same token, thanks to technology and the internet, it's unnecessary to be in the same room or country as your mentor. Face-to-face and group coaching can and do happen more frequently because of technology. You can ask questions, get counsel, gain wisdom, and follow the example and advice of a mentor in another country.

Masterminds are most effective for the end user when the protégé or mentee utilizes various mentors.

Characteristics of Good Mentors

Mastermind members challenge you to grow and face your issues.

The worst thing you can have for an effective mentor is a "yes man" or "yes woman." We all need to be challenged to change, think, and grow. If we surround ourselves with "yes" people who are afraid to tell us the truth in love, we are doomed to failure.

Mastermind members celebrate your wins with you.

Mastermind members don't always know they are in your mastermind. This is especially true when your mentor lives in a different country or century than you.

Mastermind members can be of any age or education level.

I'll never forget, and I often tell the story of winning the championship baseball league when I was 14 with a 17-year-old baseball coach. Our head coach quit in mid-season, and David Johnson, who had been assistant baseball coach, took over as head coach. Of course, parents were skeptical, but my teammates and I knew not only was David a great baseball player, but David also had the respect of our entire team and knew baseball inside and out. He not only took us to win the league championship, but we also did it with only eight players!

In baseball, you're supposed to have nine players; this means that every time that 9th "ghost batter" got up to bat, we got an automatic "out," yet, even with this handicap, we went on to win the championship game in overtime. It felt like the victory of a lifetime! I didn't even mention that I was two years younger than everyone on my team. All the teams we played because my mom required the coach to put me on the same team as my brother. Since we lived so far out in the sticks, that was the only way my parents could justify my brother playing baseball in the same league as me! We became one powerful mastermind, let me tell you!

Don't limit yourself by thinking you can't learn from a child. You may even want to have a teen on your board or your executive committee; particularly if you want your message to impact millennials, you'll want to have more than one young person on your advisory board.

You can win from the advice and counsel of others from your mastermind, even if they are no longer living and no matter what age.

Mastermind members should be a diverse group of people.

Women think differently than men, which is one reason my mom is still in my mastermind. Even though some of her ideas and methods drive me crazy, her wisdom and input have proven invaluable over the years. I have people from different countries, different upbringings, different mindsets, different genders, different life experiences, and different industries who make up my ever-growing and revolving door to my mastermind.

Mastermind members should be changed out periodically.

"When I was a child, I spoke as a child, I understood as a child, I thought as a child; but when I became a man, I put away childish things."
~ I Corinthians 13: 11

If you're growing and maturing in business and in life, you'll want to fire or graduate your mentors out of your life. There's a real-time place to thank them and then cut them loose. You can do this with honor and dignity, never out of anger or out of an emotional reaction.

How do you know when it is that time to let a mentor go? When they're no longer stretching you, challenging you, and helping you grow. When you always pull them forward, and they no longer challenge you to be your best, it's time to cut the string and move on.

Replace them with someone stronger, wiser, and more successful than the previous mentor, giving them space to grow and move on personally. This is good for all three of you, the former mentor, the new mentor, and you and your entire organization.

I can't wait to see who you've selected as your mastermind members!

MICHAEL D. BUTLER

About Michael D. Butler: Called the Simon Cowell of Book Publishing, celebrity kingmaker Michael Butler is most proud of his 4 sons and 2 grandsons. His authors have spoken in 50 countries.

As a global book publisher and speaker Butler is a recognized authority in the book publishing space. Helping authors and speakers evolve and create platforms of influence in an ever-changing marketplace.

Author's Website: *www.MichaelDButler.com*

Book Series Website & Author's Bio: *www.The13StepsToRiches.com*

Michelle Cameron Coulter & Allan Coulter

FURTHER TOGETHER

"We have the opportunity to go further together...and it's a lot more fun."
By Michelle Cameron Coulter and Allan Coulter

As we write this, I am about to jump into the biggest investment I have ever made to join a mastermind.

The truth is masterminds are the most powerful way to leverage and condense time as far as sourcing resources and surrounding oneself with others who are playing bigger.

The sum of the parts is always much greater than anything we can do alone.

One of the biggest misconceptions is that as leaders and entrepreneurs, we think we "need" to be able to do it on our own, and often lone wolf it.

The truth is we go faster and further together, and it's a heck of a lot more fun too! When involved in a mastermind, that feeling of "being alone" while running your business or project is gone. Other members of the group turn into advisors of sorts and vice versa.

Collaboration is the name of the game. You may find someone in the group that is a perfect fit to work on a project with you. Or, you may be the perfect person to help another member. The group works together collaboratively to achieve more together.

Masterminds are an opportunity to extend your network. Being part of a mastermind expands your network exponentially and rapidly. If you are in business, you know how important your network is. By joining a mastermind, you instantly add to your network and typically gain the networks of those in the group.

It is a huge opportunity to learn and grow. Everyone in a mastermind is unique in skill, experience, and connections. By interacting and sharing your challenges, it's almost certain that someone in your mastermind will have a solution for you. You may also be able to offer a solution, connection, or tactic to help another in the group.

It is an opportunity to cross-promote. When you join a mastermind, you will most likely find ways to help each other by utilizing cross-promotion, supporting each other, and finding ways to help each other through promoting to your respective networks.

Expand your perspective and think bigger. Being in a mastermind will truly give you a Master Mind! You can't help but think bigger and stretch beyond your boundaries when surrounded by amazing people doing amazing things.

One of the most amazing experiences that came out of a Mastermind-like environment we shared a few years ago.

We were invited to travel to a poor area of Mexico just outside of Tijuana. There was no way anyone in this area could even dream of ever owning a home. We came in with a group of friends and colleagues, not knowing what to expect.

Al, being from the home building industry, knew the fastest he had ever seen a home built was 3 months. Now we have watched "Extreme Home Makeover," where they could build a home in a week. In this case, we were coming in to help out for three days.

It was a very interesting process as we all met the first evening and were divided into teams depending on our skills. The next day we were taken out to the site, and to our surprise, we were going to be building three homes. Now we found out that these homes would equal the size of a double car garage in North America, which normally would still take a week to build one.

This was where the teamwork and masterminding came together: one group was cutting wood, the next was framing, and another was painting and trim work. Finally, there was still another group in charge of shopping for all the items to go inside the house.

Watching everyone working as a team and the structures go up was so cool. The really neat part was inside the working of the Mastermind; it actually got a little competitive for which group got the roof on first. Also, if a group fell behind, the other groups would jump in to help to a point where we were way ahead of what the leaders thought we would get done for the day.

We remember coming to the site on the second day after the buildings were framed on the first day and feeling so proud of what we had accomplished. On the second day, we worked hard, got the roofs shingled, all the wood painted, and installed the windows and doors. After finishing the trim work and painting, the group arrived with all the furniture, beds, and necessities. It was incredible teamwork, and because we were ahead of schedule, we had time to build window flower boxes and special trim around the front door.

By far, the most powerful part of the whole experience was the ceremony for handing the keys over to the families that were moving in and working alongside us through this process. There was not a dry eye in the place, and the family came around, hugged each of us, and thanked us for our hard work.

It was an amazing Mastermind experience that we will never forget.

If you ever get the opportunity, we recommend jumping in with both feet.

The power of a mastermind and the magic that can be created has the potential to be compounded beyond measure.

MICHELLE CAMERON COULTER & AL COULTER

About Michelle Cameron Coulter: Michelle is an Olympic gold medalist, entrepreneur, mother of four, community leader raising millions of dollars for charities, global inspirational leader, and founder and CEO of Inspiring Possibilities.

About Al Coulter: Al is a two-time Olympian in volleyball, captain of Team Canada, world record holder in matches representing one's country in any sport, with over 735 matches, entrepreneur, father of four, and personal best coach, specializing in relationships, team, and resilience.

Michelle and Al are the embodiment of today's leaders. Strong and empowering, they embraced life's challenges with strength and courage. They bring insight, compassion, depth, and inspiration to the table with multiple world championships, three Olympics, an Olympic gold medal, marriage, and four children.

They are sought-after inspirational leaders. Through their speaking, workshops, and retreats, their gift and passion is to "inspire possibilities" and supports people to embrace their greatness in a real, authentic, healthy, and vibrant way—creating thriving community, connection, and one's own gold medal results.

Author's website: *www.MichelleCameronCoulter.com*
Book Series Website & Author's Bio: *www.The13StepsToRiches.com*

Michelle Mras

THE MULTIPLIER OF ABUNDANCE

*"Belonging is one of the most basic needs that every person has...
If you desire to be a better leader, develop an other-person mindset.
Begin looking for ways to include others."*
~ John C. Maxwell, Becoming A Person of Influence

Do you consider yourself a lone wolf? Many small business owners and entrepreneurs tend to begin with that thought in mind. I know I did. I set out alone when I began my professional speaking and leadership coaching business years ago. My pack was the Toastmasters International family and political campaign circles. They both work in groups to achieve goals and win elections. So, when I declared I was going to take this speaking show on the road, I was told, "good luck" and patted on the back...a lone wolf without a pack to fall back upon. It was terrifying to set my sights on various speaking engagements knowing that I had to rely on my brain power, intuition, business skills, past experiences, and ability to adapt. No one I knew had walked this path of professional speaking.

I quickly realized that I needed something beyond my stellar speaking skills. I needed a product beyond myself. Did I figure that out by myself? Not at all! I learned it from a friend who invited me to join the John Maxwell Team (JMT) of certified coaches. I joined a pack closer in alignment with my professional speaking lane. He was my first co-wolf. Once I attended the JMT certification, my pack grew immensely! These were people, new family, that also had aspirations to grow as professional speakers. We would talk late into the night about our shared experiences in professional speaking and, soon, the coaching world. The ability to share knowledge with those who had "been there, done that" and provide insight from my cultural and specific educational background was a catalyst for the immense growth of my business. This interaction served me for several years, and I built strong bonds with a few of the coaches. We still meet to bounce ideas and share acquired knowledge in our perspective fields.

One day, one of my close JMT coaching friends said, "I wish we could bring our Mastermind back together." I responded, "What Mastermind?" He responded with laughter, "What do you think we were doing on our calls? We were a Mastermind group." My mind had never considered what we did together a Mastermind. We just shared what we learned through experience, education, or intuition. I had coined the meetings as our Wolf Pack time. In *Think and Grow Rich*, Napoleon Hill described the Mastermind principle as "The coordination of knowledge and effort between two or more people who work towards a definite purpose in a spirit of harmony…no two minds ever come together without thereby creating a third, invisible, intangible force, which may be likened to a third mind". My fellow coach and friend enlightened me about the concept of a Mastermind.

"You are the average of the five people you spend the most time with."
~ Jim Rohn

That was my introduction to Masterminds. I had been in one that set my business afloat, and I had no idea. I became a part of yet another Mastermind with a group of coaches that attended a retreat

with Dr. Paul Scheele of Scheele Learning Systems. Wowzah! What an amazing experience. People from all walks of life, countries, and age groups came together with the goal of accelerating better outcomes for our professional and personal lives. Together we helped envision and create paths for our success. This was a new level of Mastermind. In this group,

I realized that diversity of background was essential to massive growth. Through the years, the group is still together. A few have come and gone, but the core still remains.

More recently, I became associated with a man I met by coincidence at the Ultimate Speaker Competition in Orlando, Florida. While I was in the middle of the competition, he approached me and complimented my speaking and storytelling skills. I thanked him and continued with the speaking competition. Later, he approached me again to invite me to be in a book called the DOSE of HOPE for his 501c3 KEEP SMILING Movement. I agreed, wrote my chapter, and submitted it. He then requested time to speak with me via Zoom. When we got on the video call, something shifted. He shared what his book was about and why he wanted me to submit a story. I shared more about my background and the short story I submitted for the book.

There was a different level of synergy that occurred. We were in alignment with what we wished to bring to the world. I believe everyone has a story that must be shared regardless of how "not tragic" or "tragic." There is someone waiting to hear that someone else experienced what they experienced or that the world is not as horrible as social media shows us. The people of the world need HOPE (Hold On Pain Ends). We both believe that this can be done one story at a time. I share my stories, written and spoken. He helps people build a legacy by publishing those stories in collaboration books for more exposure. Double WOWZAH!

Since this meeting, we have become co-creators of Ampifluence - Amplify Your Influence - "You're the Expert, but are you struggling to monetize your Authority?" This has become the ultimate Mastermind, in my opinion. We travel across the United States and, soon, abroad to meet with authors, speakers, coaches, and influencers from all areas of business to share their authority with the people in their own areas, highlight them in a book based on their geographic area and share thoughts, missions and growth plans to expand their circle into other geographic areas. We Amplify who they are and tie them to other influencers, so we all grow our influence together. The beauty of this system and process is that we have created Masterminds in each geographic area, then tie them to the next geographic area. In essence, we are building satellite Mastermind groups that tie to one larger Amplifluence Mastermind!

I discovered through this process with my co-founder, Ken Rochon, known as "Dr. Smiley," that a Mastermind does not require a large group to be effective. The two of us were a Mastermind that developed and grew our individual businesses exponentially and drew on our satellite Mastermind groups to collaborate when we saw a possibility of collaboration. As a result, there has been massive growth amongst those who have joined us in this endeavor. We are constantly expanding and acquiring more people into our Amplifluence Mastermind family.

My question to you is, "Who are you masterminding with?" It can be anyone who doesn't think like you. Who is a good candidate: your spouse, friend, associate, networking partner, or like, in my case, a person you randomly meet at a speaking competition. The key is to bring minds together with different skill sets, perspectives, and positive mindsets. Thoughts you have had and have brushed off as unworkable can be heard by another, refined, and become exactly what you were seeking. You just need another set of brain cells to examine it. Together, you can polish the idea to make it a gem. Start with two people, then expand. Build your third master brain.

"1+1=11!"
~ Sharon Lechter, Think and Grow Rich for Women

ABOUT MICHELLE MRAS

About Michelle Mras: Michelle is a Global Award-Winning Keynote & TEDx Speaker, Presentation Coach, co-Host of two podcasts: Denim & Pearls and Amplifluence. Michelle is the Host of MentalShift on The New Channel (TNC), Philippines. She's a multiple Best-Selling Author and co-Founder of Amplifuence - Amplifying the influence of Coaches, Authors and Speakers.

Michelle is a survivor of multiple life challenges to include a Traumatic Brain Injury and Breast Cancer. She guides others to recognize the innate gifts within them, stop apologizing for what they are not and step into who they truly are… Unapologetically.

Author's Website: *www.MichelleMras.com*
Book Series Website & Author's Bio: *www.The13StepsToRiches.com*

Mickey Stewart

ANGELS IN MY ATTIC

There I was, standing in the Royal Box, seeking shelter from the freezing January rain that fell upon the rest of the outdoor film set that was a grand, 17th-century stately Scottish home. It was 3 am, yet I was buzzing with energy as my body was still on LA time after finishing Leadership training there. My face ached from smiling, not just from shooting the same takes over and over, from every possible angle, but from the gratifying knowledge I had once again co-created with the Master Mind.

I have been trying to embody the 13 Steps to Riches that Napoleon Hill shared in *Think and Grow Rich* since first discovering this incredible book in 2008, not just to become financially abundant but to live a rich and full life that overflows with magical adventures and interactions. This recent filming experience was another piece of evidence I had just collected to prove to myself that these principles worked. But, this time, it was tapping into the POWER of the Master Mind.

> "No two minds ever come together without, thereby, creating a third, invisible, intangible force which may be likened to a third mind."
> ~ Napoleon Hill

The Power of the Master Mind is the ultimate example of Co-Creation and a chain of support I tap into regularly through two avenues:

- **Worldly Mastermind**
- **Universal Master Mind**

A **Worldly Mastermind** is with humans living on earth in the same lifetime as you, meeting in person or virtually. My Worldly Mastermind is the intelligent and supportive group of women I met through Leadership training. We've gathered every week for two years, and although we have yet to meet in person, they are among my best friends and strongest supporters.

We start our Zoom meetings with someone taking the lead to ground us, closing our eyes for a breathing exercise or short, guided grounding process. Then we share our wins of the week and ask how we can support each other. If anyone is playing small or shrinking back from their declarations, we call each other up and stretch one another to take action outside our comfort zones. As we wrap up, we state what we are committing to for the next week and share how the group can best support us.

Tuesdays at 4 pm have become one of my favorite times of the week because I now have my own team of thought leaders cheering me on and keeping me accountable to my big visions: it's not a gift everyone has. If you're not already in one, I encourage you to seek out a mastermind group or start your own. Choose your members wisely and remember the words of Jim Rohn: 'You become the average of the five people you spend the most time with.'

The **Universal Master Mind** (spelled differently on purpose) is something BIGGER. It is Co-Creation with non-physical energy. I sometimes call it God, but I feel more connected when I make it more personal and familiar. Referring collectively to them as my Angels in my attic, there are three people who have influenced me and are significant to me. They are my dad (singer-songwriter Sonny Pero), self-development author Dr. Wayne Dyer, and frame drummer Layne Redmond. Napoleon Hill referred to his imaginary team of mentors, made of enlightened beings, dead or alive, as his Invisible Counselors.

Each morning, I walk into our third-floor attic studio and say out loud, 'Good morning, Angels.' I immediately smile because I feel supported and guided. Without fail, whenever I am working on a creative project and ask them for help, an idea or solution comes to me almost instantly. How well this works blows my mind each time and has me laughing and saying, 'Thank you, Angels' or 'Thanks, Dad.'

I think of this Universal Master Mind much like the two-way conversation I would have with my Worldly Mastermind members. First, ask for guidance and then listen for the answer, with the reply often coming through a nudge, feeling, or intuitive knowing.

On November 29th, 2020, I got up at 6 am to meet with one of my Leadership coaches, Des, who was on California time. She wanted to get to know me better and discover what made me tick. At the end of the call, she had me stretch myself to declare something BIG—on top of the big goal I was already working on. I was still groggy from just waking up and felt a bit put on the spot by someone I didn't yet know very well, but I felt like she got me. When she asked what I wanted to declare, I said, 'To publish my book by October 2021.' Then she said, 'What else?' I started laughing because I couldn't think of anything, but the next thing I knew, the following words flowed from my mouth, "I want to be in another movie by the end of this course, January 26th, 2021."

I had co-authored an international best-selling book in 2013 with twenty-one other women, but I felt called to write more. So, FIVE MONTHS after declaring that to Des, I became part of this book project and have since added SEVEN more international best-selling books to my repertoire.

My second declaration of being in a movie and how it ties into co-creating with the Master Mind, well, here's what happened.

It was Thursday, January 21st, 2021, and my body sighed with relief as my online yoga teacher said my favorite words, 'It's now time for relaxation.' I bustled around like a cat getting its bed ready with pillows and furry blankets, excitedly wondering if I'd see the purple haze that sometimes appears around my third eye during relaxation. While I drifted into deep serenity, I thought I would play with something I had recently heard about being playfully particular and demanding when requesting support from God, your Guides, and the Master Mind.

In my head, I started speaking directly to my dad. I wanted to film another movie, but all of Scotland was still in lockdown, and I didn't know if projects were even filming. Nevertheless, with my January 26th deadline fast approaching, I asked anyway. I said in my most demanding internal voice ever. 'Dad, I REALLY want that Netflix movie.' (My NDA prevents me from naming the movie.) I playfully added, 'Do you hear me, Dad? Ok? You GOT it?' And then I went into a daydream state, imagining myself in costume, getting my hair and make-up done, and being on set.

I ALWAYS turn my phone off during yoga, but I forgot that day. As I opened my eyes and sat up for the final part of the class, I noticed a text from my agent. When I saw it was for a TV show, not MY MOVIE, I mentally shouted, 'No, Dad! I don't want THAT one. I want the NETFLIX movie,' and left it at that. When an availability request comes in, you have to respond to it as soon as possible, but not long after yoga, I was released from the TV gig before I even had a chance to reply. That NEVER happens.

Later that afternoon, I got another message from my agent asking if I was available, this time for MY MOVIE! By the very next day, I was BOOKED!

Seven days after my request and two days after my declared deadline, I was driving to set with tears of gratitude in my eyes and my heart bursting with joy. Not just for the experience I was about to have but, more importantly, because of how close I felt to my dad sixteen years after he had passed.

After I had been through costume, hair, and make-up, one of the hair supervisors came over, looked at me ponderingly, and said, 'Let's try this.' I felt like I was instantly teleported into an episode of The Big Bang Theory: having an Amy Farrah Fowler moment as she placed a glistening tiara upon my head.

As we took our places on set, the Director set his eye on us, glanced up to the Royal Box, and then looked back and said, 'Let's take the four guards out of the box and put in four of these guys.' I immediately KNEW he would choose me. I had a mental flash of Dad being in the Director's head, planting the idea that said, 'Pick her.'

Before I knew it, I was among the main cast, being highly featured in MY NETFLIX MOVIE, with the costume department attaching fancy jewels to my sash to make me look more 'Royal' and touching up my lipstick.

Whether you experience the mind-blending that comes with aligning yourself with like-minded fellow humans here on the physical plane or a more psychic, intuitive alliance that happens in the spiritual realm, we, and the minds from our Worldly Mastermind and Universal Master Mind, together create the THIRD MIND: the mothership of CO-CREATION and SUPPORT.

Play with it.

MICKEY STEWART

About Mickey Stewart: Born in Cape Breton, Canada, Mickey Stewart is a musician, coach, and author who has been a player and instructor of the snare drum and bodhrán for forty years. Responsible for heading up the drum program at Ardvreck School in Perthshire, Scotland since 2002, Mickey is in high demand to teach throughout the U.K. and North America.

Creator and founder of BodhránExpert.com, her YouTube videos have received more than two million views from students and fans from every country throughout the world.

Over the past eight years, she's been involved in the TV and film industry as a supporting artist. Even more recently, she's begun following her newest passion, which is teaching others how to share their talents with the world.

Stewart lives in Crieff, Scotland with her husband of twenty-five years, Scottish musician and composer Mark Stewart, along with their 17-year-old son, Cameron, who is also a piper.

Author's Website: *www.MickeyStewart.com*
Book Series Website & Author's Bio: *www.The13StepsToRiches.com*

Natalie Susi

MASTERMIND MAGIC

Starting, running, and building a business is hard. Creating a partnership with someone and navigating life's ups and downs is also hard. Making money most efficiently and effectively doing the thing that lights you up on the planet is pretty hard to navigate at first, too. Creating a space where you are consistently successful in achieving your desires in life and work is a big feat, and it shouldn't be done alone. Life and business are not meant to be done alone. We need people, like minds, accountability, and constructive feedback to help us move through all of the lessons and experiences that life throws at us. This is where the magic of masterminds comes into play.

Let me explain a bit more.

Have you ever had a plan or desire that is taking up space in your head but not in your real life? In other words, do you think about it often but don't actually take the physical steps to bring it to life? Maybe you have a business you've always wanted to start or a relationship you want to call in. Maybe you want to attract more clients or finally develop that app you keep telling everyone about. Perhaps you've taken the time to write the business plan, but you've gotten stuck on how to raise the money, or you're too scared to start telling people about your next big idea. We have all been there. Great ideas. Great intentions. No real action steps or partial action steps that get dwarfed and halted by fear, indecision, or excuses about not having enough time and energy. I totally get it. I've been there for many ideas and many moments in my life.

I used to wonder how I could turn my desires into reality all of the time. They all seemed so far out of reach. I struggled with a mindset of lack. As I've shared in previous books, I had the desire to sell my first business in the food and beverage industry, but I didn't really know how to expand beyond what I had already accomplished. This was my first business, and I learned most of my lessons the hard way. I wore every single hat in the business right down to delivering the product out of the back of my Hyundai. At the time, I didn't feel like I had enough money, knowledge, and/or opportunities to truly create the desired outcome and sell the company. I eventually realized that the issue wasn't a lack of resources. It was a lack of a supportive team of people who could advise me and give me insights on the next best steps to achieve my desired outcome.

The proactive step to support in moments like these is starting a mastermind group. In the classic book, *Think and Grow Rich*, Napoleon Hill introduces the mastermind concept as "The coordination of knowledge and effort of two or more people, who work toward a definite purpose, in the spirit of harmony…No two minds ever come together without thereby creating a third, invisible, intangible force, which may be likened to a third mind [the master mind]." He encouraged people to gather together in a structured, repeatable environment for the success of all.

Mastermind groups offer a combination of brainstorming, education, peer accountability, and support to sharpen your business and personal skills. A mastermind group helps you and your members succeed, and they serve as catalysts for growth. A mastermind is a cumulation of a cooperative alliance that will produce more money and knowledge than one person ever could. The group requires commitment and a desire to create mutually beneficial, nonjudgmental, harmonious relationships where there is an even energetic exchange of time, energy, and constructive feedback and support. Organizing your efforts and coming together as a collective result in the power of transformation.

Once I started implementing the mastermind principle in my life, my business began to expand, I started to learn how to do things more efficiently and effectively, and I developed more genuine, authentic relationships with fellow entrepreneurs with complementary skillsets and relatable stories. I was engaging in meaningful, helpful, and informative conversations, and I started seeing the positive impact in my life, my business, and my bank account. I sold my first company, Bare Organic Mixers, 6 months after engaging in my first mastermind. I started my next service-based company for coaching and consulting and finally stepped back into the kind of work I wanted to do on the planet. I was making more money than I ever thought I could see as a service-based business owner. I attribute much of these wins to the mastermind principle. This group of people helped me stay aligned with my vision and provided a safe space for me to learn, grow, and make mistakes. We all experienced wins and losses together.

Mastermind groups can produce infinite intelligence, accumulated experience, and experiment and research that is valuable beyond measure. Tapping into the knowledge of others to help further assist us with our goals works like magic. We often learn more by speaking less and listening more. As Hill says, when two like-minded people share experiences and sincere advice, it inevitably creates a "third mind," enabling the psychic phase of the mastermind. This is where creativity pours out, and abundance starts flowing into both lives. This also unlocks the door to infinite intelligence and allows the universe to work its magic in these conversations and relationships. This can be done effortlessly since the connection between the two is authentic and made with the right intentions. Ultimately, this is the greatest source of power that one could have since it reaches the highest level of "genius."

To tie all of these pieces together, I had to trade in my original lack mindset for an abundance mindset. In life, there are two streams we can take, which also affect our sources of income. The first is a positive stream that requires a strong-minded thinking process in the beliefs of optimism and attraction to the great things in life. This will lead to fortune, success, and accomplishments regardless of hardships in our path. The other stream embodies a negative mindset that leads to poverty, misery, and regret. It is filled with judgment and frustration. I often ask myself, "Which stream am I going to choose for myself?" "The one with an abundance of wealth, opportunity, and happiness, or the one with regret, shame, and poverty?"

Before you begin each day, ask yourself which stream would fulfill your desires most effectively. What kind of life do you want to create for yourself? One switch in your mindset can switch your entire reality. Poverty does not need power, organized knowledge, a mastermind, a third mind, or infinite intelligence. All it needs is doubt since its boldness is intimidating. Yet riches are often viewed as wishful thinking. This is far from the truth. Riches come from a definite plan, a strong community, and a burning desire for wealth and success. Ask yourself which life you would rather pursue, and then sit down and start planning the next steps to take you there. Make sure one of them is joining a mastermind. Check out the below simple exercises if you'd like some support in getting started.

EXERCISE:

- Describe where you desire to be in three years
- Get clear on how much money you desire to make and what you're going to do to earn it
- Consider if you are leveraging the power of the Master Mind principle in your life. If not, who could you connect with regularly to help you take an area of your life to the next level?
- Start your first mastermind with at least 2-3 participants

NATALIE SUSI

About Natalie Susi: Natalie has more than 14 years of experience as a teacher, speaker, entrepreneur and mentor. Currently she's a 5-year UCSD professor focusing on communications and the Pursuit of Happiness. As an entrepreneur, she founded and grew Bare Organic Mixers beverage company for 8 years resulting in an acquisition in 2014.

After selling the company, Natalie combined her educational background as a teacher and her experience as an entrepreneur to provide personal development coaching and consulting to individuals, businesses, and creative entrepreneurs. She develop a program called Conscious Conversations and utilizes a step-by-step process called The Alignment Method to support leaders in cultivating conscious teams and businesses through a process of self-reflection, self-discover, and self-ascension that ultimately increases profits, productivity, and the growth of the individuals, personally and professionally.

Author's website: *www.NatalieSusi.com*
Book Series Website & Author's Bio: *www.The13StepsToRiches.com*

Nita Patel

THE SECRET MASTERMIND

In October 2015, I sold my most prize possession, a two-carat diamond ring. A few weeks later, I purchased a five-figure membership to a mastermind group. <gasp> Who was I, and what was happening to me? The reason I would ever let go of something so valuable would be to upgrade it for a bigger diamond. For someone whose pride and joy were measured with sparkles, whatever possessed me to make a decision like this?

I had just read Napoleon Hill's *Think and Grow Rich* for the first time in my life. I was so intrigued by the idea of a formal mastermind group and the possibilities, or magic rather, that could come into my life as a result that maybe I could buy a bigger diamond later or something better. Something was missing in my life then, and until I figured out how to feel fulfilled, I absolutely had to commit to this. I blocked off 1.5 hours on my calendar every Tuesday morning for 13 months. I reserved a conference room so I could speak my mind without the judgment of my coworkers' eavesdropping.

At first, I didn't quite understand where the conversations were going. It felt like I had joined a support group. But given my level of investment, I had to stick to the plan to see where this was going to take me. I was desperately trying to get a promotion at work during this time. I was applying for any new job that looked of interest. I constantly told myself that I couldn't have any of these positions because there was only one job, and clearly, it was meant for someone else. How could I possibly be promoted when someone else was better qualified, experienced, and, well, they probably deserved it more than I did anyway. After all, I felt like a fraud expecting to be promoted for a job I wasn't sure I was great at despite the facts.

One day I was listening to Bob Proctor while driving, and I heard him say a famous quote from the Upanishads. "From abundance came abundance, and abundance remains." I thought to myself, that's interesting in theory. Sure doesn't sound practical, though. Then I listened to him further explain how two people in a room taking deep breaths doesn't take any oxygen away from a third person who enters and breathes. Wait, what? That actually sounds like it makes sense. If I breathe, I'm not taking oxygen away from anyone else. That much I could grasp with ease. As I broke down the explanation in my own words, it made much more sense.

God is abundant; therefore, so is His universe where I reside. Oxygen is abundant, and so is water, food, beauty in nature, and all the emotions I want to experience at my own will. The more analogies I came up with, the more I understood the power of an abundant world. The more I learned about the laws of the universe, the more I understood how my world worked. I then learned about the power of my thoughts and words and how they impacted my life. No wonder I wasn't getting any of the jobs I applied for. I thought they were already allocated to someone more deserving than me. I assumed that I wouldn't get the job; therefore, I wouldn't. With the idea of abundance, I could have anything I wanted. At this moment, my whole world changed. I started scripting for all the things that I wanted. Suddenly the desperation of being promoted faded as I stepped into a much bigger world of possibilities. Ironically, I got the promotion shortly after that and with ease.

I attributed this newfound philosophy to my mastermind group. I could've read the same content over and over, but it wasn't until I joined this exclusive group that had the same goals, I had that my whole life changed. All of our lives were changing before our own eyes, and the beautiful thing was we were witnesses to each other's successes. None of this could've happened at the rate and intensity at which it was happening had it not been for the mastermind group. Every few weeks, my mind expanded to new higher consciousness concepts. I developed a deep desire to continue learning. The more familiar I became with the mastermind; I realized I could have more than one mastermind. I continued my journey of masterminding in many areas of life. Academics, spirituality, business, and creativity. Each conversation expanded my mind to a level of possibilities I could never see before. Through this, my health and relationships improved, and I found a new and aligned purpose through my creativity. My life became unrecognizable to the 'me' I used to know. In fact, I've never worn a diamond since that day. My true joy now comes from being creative and learning. Who needs diamonds when you're busy applying the Fibonacci sequence to a painting or learning to use quantum physics to heal through artwork. No amount of carats can be traded for a painting with that power. In conclusion, I'd like to leave you with a few of my thoughts on your mastermind journey.

Here are some basic rules for a mastermind to ensure you are in an authentic and elevating space.

1. Only pay for a mastermind if you're going to get elite access to successful thought leaders on a regular basis. Don't pay someone to be in their mastermind where all you get is people selling their services to you. That is NOT a real mastermind. A real mastermind is there to support you unselfishly. Many businesses have monetized the concept of a mastermind these days, and it's all to support the group's owner in buying their services and supporting their mission. This is not going to support your growth and personal development.

2. The most successful masterminds are those where people from different backgrounds, industries, and goals come together

to support one another. This often works best as it eliminates competition. Collaboration is the key to success. Competition and collaboration cannot co-exist. When each person in your group is focused on a different goal from a different industry, there is no room for competition, thus enabling success.

3. Don't sacrifice your values to be in a group that you believe will elevate you. This can be a disguise for many things, ultimately derailing you from your ultimate goals. We have work to do and no time to waste. So keep your eyes and ears open.

4. The right group will make you feel excited and elevated and push you beyond your comfort zone if you allow it. You will need immediate progress when you join this group, both within yourself and the world around you.

5. Keep it simple. Three people or more is a perfect place to start. Like-minded individuals will keep this group harmonious and easy to meet with. Mix it up – phone calls, zoom calls, and in-person visits to maximize the energy of the group. A set schedule for a prolonged period can become mundane and lose energy after a while. Keep your interactions fresh and energetic.

Above all, have fun! No success can be achieved without having fun. And if you do, where's the fun in that!

NITA PATEL

About Nita Patel: Nita is a best-selling author, speaker, and artist who believes in modern etiquette as a path to becoming our best selves.

Through her professional years, Ms. Patel has 25 years of demonstrated technology leadership experience in various industries specifically with a concentrated focus in health care for 14 of those 20+ years. She's shown her art across the world to include the Louvre in Paris. She's a best-selling author and performance coach, pursuing her master's in industrial organizational (I-O) psychology at Harvard. Her investment in psychology theory and practice is what led her to a deep interest in helping others. She has become deeply and passionately devoted to nurturing others and in building their confidence and brand through speaking and consultative practices.

Author's Website: *www.Nita-Patel.com*
Book Series Website & Author's Bio: *www.The13StepsToRiches.com*

Olga Geidane

DEFITINITE PURPOSE ACHIEVED IN A MASTERMIND

"Mr. Carnegie's Master Mind Group consisted of a staff of approximately 50 individuals with whom he surrounded himself for the DEFINITE PURPOSE of manufacturing and marketing steel. He attributed his entire fortune to the POWER he accumulated through this Master Mind."

~Napoleon Hill, Think and Grow Rich

"Great power can be accumulated through no other principle!"

~Napoleon Hill, Think and Grow Rich

"Nature's building blocks are available to humanity in the energy involved in THINKING! The human brain may be compared to an electric battery. It absorbs energy from what may be called "The Mysterious Unifying Force of the Universe," which permeates every atom of matter—including the atoms that compose the human brain—and fills the entire universe."

~Napoleon Hill, Think and Grow Rich

OLGA GEIDANE

About Olga Geidane: Olga is an International Speaker, an Event MC/Host, Facilitator, Mindset Coach, a Best-Selling Author, and a Regional President of the Professional Speaking Association in the UK. She is a host of Olga's Show and A World-Traveler.

Olga helps ambitious people to unlock their extraordinary performance and their true, authentic side. She is passionate about helping people to live their best lives. Olga knows how tough it is to be broke and unfulfilled in life: at the age of 24, just after her divorce, Olga came to the UK from Latvia with no spoken English, with just £100 in her pocket, and a 2.5-year-old son. Olga is a very inspirational survivor: she went through abuse, betrayal, cheating, financial loss, and emotional breakdown. Matt Black (Business Model Innovation & Disruption Consultant—Snr. Advisor to CEO CSO CCO COO—Author & International Public Speaker) said: "Olga really takes it up a notch beyond anything I have seen before. She is one of the bravest people I have ever seen on stage. If you are looking to book a speaker or attend a talk that will be inspiring, challenging, and leave you wanting to take action... She is perfect."

Author's Website: *www.OlgaGeidane.com*
Book Series Website & Author's Bio: *www.The13StepsToRiches.com*

Paul Capozio

TWO MINDS CAN CREATE A THIRD

"TO THINK HEALTH WHEN SURROUNDED BY THE APPEARANCES OF DISEASE, OR TO THINK RICHES WHEN IN THE MIDST OF APPEARANCES OF POVERTY, REQUIRES POWER; BUT HE WHO ACQUIRES THIS POWER BECOMES A MASTER MIND. HE CAN CONQUER FATE; HE CAN HAVE WHAT HE WANTS."

~*Wallace D. Wattles*

"NO TWO MINDS EVER COME TOGETHER WITHOUT, THEREBY, CREATING A THIRD INVISIBLE, INTANGIBLE FORCE WHICH MAY BE LIKENED TO A THIRD MIND."

~*Napoleon Hill, Think And Grow Rich*

"A GROUP OF BRAINS COORDINATED IN A SPIRIT OF HARMONY WILL PROFIDE MORE THOUGH- ENERGY THAN A SINGLE BRAIN, JUST AS A GROUP OF BATTERIES WILL PROVIDE MORE ENERGY THAN A SINGLE BATTERY."

~*Napoleon Hill, Think And Grow Rich*

PAUL CAPOZIO

About Paul Capozio: Paul Capozio was born in Hoboken, New Jersey, and grew up on the streets of Hudson County. At 35, he was recruited to be the President of Sales and Marketing for a 350-million-dollar human resources firm. In 7 years, he drove the top-line revenue of that firm to over 1.5 billion.

Capozio owns and operates Capco Capital, Inc., an investment and consulting firm. The majority of Capco's holdings are of manufacturers and distributors of health and wellness products and human resources firms. Capco provides sales consulting and training, helping companies increase sales through traditional and direct sales disciplines. Making the invisible visible and simplifying the complex is his stock and trade.

A dynamic public speaker, he provides motivation and "meat and potatoes" skills to those in the health and wellness field who do not consider themselves "salespeople," allowing their voices to be heard above the "noise.

He is a husband of 32 years to his wife, Linda. He is also a father and grandfather.

Author's Website: *www.PaulCapozio.com*
Purchase Book Online: www.*The13StepsToRiches.com*

Phillip McClure

MAKING A MASTERMIND

The value of surrounding yourself with people whose ambitions and goals align with your own is critical for your success. These people are not always in the same field but often have the same mindset regarding motivation, inspiration, and goal attainment. It is up to you to find these people. Below is what I have done to be successful in the surrounding of mentors and people of influence who have been there for me every step of the way.

Pick something, anything you want to do. Find a place to do it, find other people that want to do the same thing. Then invest. This investment will be primarily your time; it is up to you to create the time necessary for your desired outcome.

The exotic car community's age fluctuates from 19 to 80 years old. I remember some young men, probably in their early twenties, asking another young man around the same age how he could buy a half-million-dollar car. The successful man asked them straight up if they were getting up at 4 am. They both said no. He then said, "Start getting up at four am then, and come see me in six months and tell me what you have learned." Once you have decided to make more time to invest in yourself, you will get the results that people only dream of because they are asleep. I start my day at 0345 and accomplish more by 1000 because of minimal distractions and not being reactive to what the day throws at me. Once that part of the day starts, I have already won by taking care of myself and moving forward in some aspects.

Once you have started learning the lingo of the subject you are working towards, you can find the people doing it. It is much easier to have your questions answered when they are not overly generalized and have some specificity. This helps you not only get the proper answers you need, but it shows appreciation to the individuals who are answering your questions. You are not wasting their time. If you're not wasting their time and energy, they are now investing in you. Be the one who is getting invested in. Show them you have put time into yourself and that you are supposed to be there.

Masterminds are not always labeled as such. We are often just naturally formed by people who want to be around people with the same goals or interests. One thing that has worked very well for me is, once I put myself into the uncomfortable arena of the unknown and being the new guy hanging around, I listen a lot. I then find the people later and ask them directed questions. If the communication goes well, I ask if they will be back again the next time everyone gets back together, as I would love to continue the conversation after I implement what they have shared with me. This is you beginning your Mastermind. You do this with two or three different people, and it is only a matter of time before you find yourselves all at the same table having these deep discussions. Congratulations, you have built the Mastermind that will help you and all the others in the group. Be sure that you find a way to bring value as well.

Bringing value to your Mastermind can be accomplished in a few different ways. By researching what the discussion left off, you can direct the next discussion by having open-ended and thought-provoking questions that will continue to drive the conversations. Boom! You have just become the Mastermind Leader. The leader does not need to know everything;

they just need to keep information flowing and passed around to each other. If you are not comfortable doing this and would rather take more of the back seat or fly on the wall stance, then project your questions to the group's natural leader and let it flow naturally from them. Bringing value does not always mean you are including your knowledge in the group; you can do this in other ways.

Just two weeks ago, I was in a situation where someone who is in my circle but is very much above my skill level and would be very difficult to get my hands on in a private setting stated he needed help painting a formula 3 car for a big presentation. I used to paint cars and jumped at the opportunity. I let him know I would be available the entire weekend, which I was not, but I was willing to create the time. He invited me to his place, and we tore apart and painted almost the entire thing in two days. I showed my value in other ways. As a reward, I received one-on-one mentorship that helped solidify my position as a circle member. This has also resulted in being invited to his homes and to dinners. The skills you possess will come in handy; do not be afraid to bring them to light. You are good at many things, and you may often believe you are not. Listen to others as they will tell you what your talents are.

People have asked me what I am good at. I like to say, "I am good at people." My upbringing of being alone in my family created the ability to make many friends and successfully chameleon into many different groups when needed. I am often asked if I know someone in a certain arena to help solve a problem or make a connection. I only recently realized that this can and should be monetized. So if you are doing this for free, look at how often you're helping a friend of a friend make a connection. It is hard at first, but simply ask, "What's it worth to you to have this connection?" 5% of sales, or maybe even access to someone else whom you would like an audience with. Keep finding ways to connect with more and more people. You never know when your value will shine or an opportunity will present itself.

There is no reason to limit yourself to simply one Mastermind. You should have many. Some will be formal; some could be as simple as a couple accountability partners that you talk to regularly to ensure you are all still on track and not drifting away from your goals. The beautiful part is you can bounce back and forth between them with valuable shared knowledge learned from other masterminds. This also allows you to show your value when someone in one group needs something. No one in that group can fulfill the gap, but you know the exact person in another mastermind that is perfect for what is needed.

I currently work with the Secret Knock Core Team mastermind. This is a powerful group of mentors, business leaders, and entrepreneurs who receive mentorship from some of the greatest business leaders around. Level Up Mastermind with Louisa Jovanovich (another author in this series) brings the most amazing guests for education and some of the best feedback you will ever find. Then finally, in the exotic car community. These meetings are never scheduled, but when a group of us meet or go to dinner together, the value is absolute. It is always in person, and you can spend more one-on-one time with people for follow-up education and information.

Find a way to become part of many masterminds. Show your value and have fun with being uncomfortable for the first little bit. This means you're growing, and you're supposed to be there. You would not be there if you had not done everything that you have done up to this point. It's just the next step, so take it and the one after. You will thank yourself later for doing so, as it will accelerate your progress.

Don't only see your dreams in your sleep. Instead, see them with open eyes and share them.

PHILLIP D. MCCLURE

About Phillip D. McClure: Phillip is married to the love of his life, Maaike McClure, and is a very proud father of two exciting kids. He was raised in the Great state of Montana before moving to Utah. Phil lives life to the fullest. His accomplishments consist completing a full Ironman, deploying four times with the Army, earning multiple decorations along the way. Including two Utah crosses! Which makes him the only soldier in history to receive that medal twice. Currently, Phil is the Owner of NorthStar Coins, Events by NorthStar, the co-owner of P.B. Fast cars and recruits pilots for the Army Aviation program. It was during his last deployment that he accidentally created his first mastermind and it has forever changed his life as well as the others involved. He mentors and coaches in self-improvement and physical fitness.

Phil is an exotic-car enthusiast who spends as much time behind the wheel as possible, whether it is carving through canyons, ripping around the racetrack, or coaching others to see their potential. Competitive driving is the best therapy in the world.

Live life to the fullest and have fun while doing it. You don't get a rewind in life so take mistakes as the lessons they are and improve, don't make the same mistakes twice.

Live in flow, not with the flow.

Authors website: *www.NorthStarCoins.com*
Book Series Website & Author's Bio: *www.The13StepsToRiches.com*

Robyn Scott

MASTER YOUR MIND!

I know there will be so many examples of the amazingness and importance of Masterminding! Napoleon Hill writes it out so perfectly! I will go with a different approach as we talk about master minds! The formula is simple. However, it is not very easy. With practice, you will get better and better at observing your thoughts and habits! That is where all these principles and steps start!

First, we are going to talk about judgment. I believe judgment is something that is distilled in us over time as we move along this journey called LIFE. Unfortunately, it starts early in life, and thank goodness we can now look at it and CHANGE IT! Judgment of others is where I am going to start. It is easy to recognize. We have ALL JUDGED! As well as being judged. From birth, we are weighed and measured and given a score on some scale that someone made up long ago. I see the importance of these types of tests, which are still putting us in categories.

I found, to my chagrin, that my mother and I bonded over gossip. It was a safe zone, I realized. If we were talking about others, we did not have to talk about ourselves; it kept everything on the surface. YIKES! It is not nice and actually feels yucky! Yet, in our minds, we do it all day long. I challenge you, dear reader, to observe when you are judging others. No blame or shame! Just be aware of your thoughts about others you come into contact with. It is SO interesting to see! As you notice and start to recognize it for yourself, you can then make a choice. Is that a true statement about that person?

In most cases, you don't have any idea. Is it helpful? Is it disdain, loathing, pity, or compassion? The thoughts we have impact others. It is the energy that they feel, not the thoughts in your head. Thank goodness, in my case! Probably good for all of us that we can not read each other's minds. I, now, look at those individuals and care bear stare them with love! I can choose to love on that soul for just a moment. Try it; it is wondrous to experience. Smiling goes a LONG way! I write about it in my first book, which I have shared a ton within the pages of this series! Play with this! It will absotively and positutely change your perspective!

The second part of the judgment is the MOST important and can be extremely difficult. Stop JUDGING YOURSELF! I mean it! Give yourself a break! YOU ARE DIVINE! YOU ARE EXACTLY WHERE YOU ARE MEANT TO BE! You are here for a reason! You do have an enormous purpose that only you can fulfill! The best part is you get to choose and develop that for yourself! The principles in *Think and Grow Rich* are correct! It applies to every aspect of our lives! Use these principles and apply them with this perspective in mind. "If you do not conquer self, you will be conquered by self," said Napoleon Hill. In the last book of *The 13 Steps to Riches*, I wrote about my persistence to accomplish my dream and vision! I have had so many failures it almost beat me down. I almost broke! Literally! Nothing new has really changed in the process, as I write this now to you. EXCEPT ME! I have changed. Where I felt despair, I now feel hope! I felt fear and doubt, but now I am in a place of knowing, and I AM APPLYING the principles to my own life in a new way, and I am here to stay! If you've experienced difficult times, forgive yourself for your mistakes or the situations you found yourself in. A dear friend reminded me that I am expecting miracles in my life. I can now see that all of those experiences ARE miracles. Love yourself more! You really do deserve to love you right here, right now!

I believe that loving ourselves is the meaning of life here on this planet. My theory, I respect all perspectives, and this is mine. One of the hardest things for me was owning my stories. Owning the responsibility for all our mistakes, failures, and the incredibly stupid things we chose to do. Looking at all of OUR mistakes can be difficult. I talked about the stories, and I recited them as a victim. It was so easy to blame others. I was offended by and over-sensitive about little benign things. My temper is what I felt most ashamed of. All the things I did when seeing red or overly harsh to those who love me the most. It is difficult to look at. And it is the most important step to look at and take responsibility for all our actions. Remember, there are A BAZILLION amazing moments and wonderful times when you are generous, kind, loving, supportive, blissful, joyous, and exuberant! Do NOT forget to look at all the *spectabulous* parts of your life as well! I promise you that the good outnumber the bad by millions! Please use all that love you have to keep you feeling warm and fuzzy about all the experiences. We deserve to forgive ourselves for our transgressions. Observing and recognizing these reactions is the greatest thing we can do to move forward. Now that we have owned our actions in all those experiences, it is time to go a little deeper. Are you ready? I knew you were! Along with owning our actions, it is very important to look at those experiences and look at them from the perspective that we created each of those experiences.

Are you still there?

Each experience is something we learned from. In life, you can be a creator or not a creator. We can not be both. You are the creators of your life; you can harness all of these delicious principles, apply them, and integrate them, and you WILL CREATE THE LIFE YOU DESIRE! I believe I created my life from the beginning to the present. My personal life coach asked me once if I could love every single experience I have had while living here on the earth. Wait, WHAT? Love ALL my experiences. Hmmm, nope, no way, no how! I have to love my experiences with abusive boyfriends?

Disloyal friends? Parasites of people using me only to be tossed aside once they got all they wanted? A sexual assault as well as the molestation I endured? NO WAY! That was my first reaction. The more I thought about it and processed what that meant for me. I had no idea how to go about loving the horrendous things I survived and the awful secrets I was so ashamed of. I kept trying to feel how I could do that! Over the course of a few months, well, years, I revisited all the experiences I hated the most. The ones that made me feel undeserving, shameful, terrified, and livid! I also believe that earth is a journey for us as eternal beings. I existed before earth, and I will exist after. How are we to understand joy without heartache? How do we know how wonderful compassion and kindness feel unless we have felt judged, ridiculed, or excluded. I would not know how supportive my husband is! I would not know how to cherish my children so dearly and deeply unless I went through being told I could never have a baby. The very best way for me to learn about unconditional love and belonging was by being adopted! Be bold and know you are perfectly who you are! I DO LOVE everything that I have experienced! I mean it! I would love for you to look back on ALL your experiences and see how much you've learned from every single one! Hindsight is 20/20! Each of those experiences has led you to where you are today! I am not the victim! I AM A CREATOR! And so are you!

Let's talk about "you"! The "you" I am going to refer to is the divine person you are. All of us are. Who are you? I believe this goes back to the first book in *The 13 Steps to Riches* series, my chapter. I have an amazing meditation that illustrates "us" and who we are. I would love to share it with you if you are interested. Message me at #robynscottinspires. You are not your labels. I always introduced myself as a mom of five. I am a wife and sister, daughter, niece, and grandchild. I am adopted, and I grew up in Englewood, Colorado, etc.

My bio was filled with all my labels. That is not WHO I am. I am those things and so much more. Those are true statements. *Absotively* and *positutely*, however, those things are not who my highest self is. I am loyal. I am trusting and see the best in everyone! I am unconditionally loving! I am radiant and kind. I care about people and who THEY truly are! My goal is to spark awareness of worth in every soul! Within the last three years, I have lost eleven people to suicide in my family and close friends. I completely understand this all too well! I have been suicidal most of my life. I didn't know where I fit in. I had so much fear that I turned to loathing who I was. Everyone reading these words, I KNOW YOU ARE NEEDED, RIGHT HERE, RIGHT NOW! Be gentle with yourself! You have been through so much and have made it through every single one! You can have all your desires!

I know without any doubt that once you apply these habits, you will get so much more out of EVERY mastermind you are a part of! Go into masterminding with a clear mind of true unconditional intentions, and you will always get exactly what you are looking for when you gather with others!

You CAN master your mind!

ROBYN SCOTT

About Robyn Scott: Robyn is the Chief Relationship Officer for Champion Circle. She manages the prospecting program for Divinely Driven Results. Scott is a Habit Finder Coach and has worked closely with the president, Paul Blanchard, at the Og Mandino Group. She is also a certified Master Your Emotions Coach through Inscape World. Scott is commonly known in professional communities as the Queen of Connection and Princess of Play. She has been working hard for the past nine years to hone her skills as a mentor and coach.

Scott strives to teach people to annihilate judgments, embrace their own stories, and empower themselves to rediscover who they truly are. Scott is an international speaker and also teaches how to present yourself on stage.

Her first book, *Bringing People Together: Rediscovering the Lost Art of Face-to-Face Connecting, Collaborating, and Creating* was released in August 2019 and was a bestseller in seven categories.

Author's website: *www.MyChampionCircle.com/Robyn-Scott*
Book Series Website & Author's Bio: *www.The13StepsToRiches.com*

Dr. Shannon Whittington

BECOMING A MASTERMIND

What is a Mastermind? Someone who knows their craft like the back of their hand. Someone who works tirelessly in pursuit of their goals. Someone who is always hungry for more and will do whatever they need to get it. A mastermind, simply put, is someone who doesn't quit, even with the odds against them.

On the path to success, you cannot simply do "well enough." You can't coast on mediocrity and expect to achieve extraordinary results; the math doesn't add up. To achieve true, long-lasting success, you must put the concept of doing the bare minimum lightyears behind you and strive to do your absolute best. And in doing so, you will eventually find that you've become a Mastermind.

How do you elevate yourself from being "good enough" to being a Mastermind? Here are a few tips that are sure to help you get there.

Have confidence in yourself

So many of us have been raised or conditioned to think negatively about ourselves. Whether we disappointed our parents, received overly harsh criticism in school or at our jobs, or dealt with toxic relationships, someone has spoken or acted in ways that have made many of us think lowly of ourselves. Unfortunately, it's so easy to carry this mentality throughout our professional careers by doing the bare minimum and procrastinating because we think we deserve mediocrity.

Newsflash: That negativity is a liar. You deserve everything your heart desires and the opportunity to turn it into a reality. You deserve to be confident in everything you do, not only to prove others who thought so little of you wrong but to also become the person you're meant to be.

One thing that I find helps boost my confidence is meditating and reciting mantras. This isn't something that you can only do occasionally or when you feel like you need it; it should be done every single day. I've found some amazing confidence-boosting meditations on YouTube that have helped me gain confidence. I utilize them even when I don't feel like I need them because my subconscious can't tell the difference. Your confidence is nearly guaranteed to skyrocket when put into practice, putting you steps closer to becoming a true Mastermind.

Study relentlessly

Remember how I said a Mastermind is always hungry? That doesn't just mean hungry for success; it means hungry to learn. Becoming a Mastermind means moving beyond knowing "just enough" about your craft; it means working every single day to master it. It means taking classes, watching videos, and streaming podcasts related to your work. It means working toward earning your Master's or even your Doctorate if you can. It means learning enough so that you're in a position to lead or teach others.

I've also realized that becoming a Mastermind means expanding your horizons beyond school, your core craft, or your passion. Ask yourself: what else am I passionate about? Maybe you like science fiction or jazz music or think owls are really neat. I highly encourage you to treat your other, less central passions with the same hunger for learning that you have in your professional life because it will make you a more well-rounded person.

It will also teach you things you may have never expected to learn in the first place. When you choose to read more science fiction or brush up on ornithology or buy jazz records you've never heard before or whatever interests you have, you choose to treat every day like an adventure.

Stay healthy and active

To become a master of your mind, you must also become a master of your body. This doesn't mean spending 2-3 hours in the gym every single day, but it does mean that you should do something that physically challenges you 4-5 days per week for around 30 minutes per day. No matter how busy we are, we are not too busy to neglect our bodies and, in turn, the mental sharpness that comes from physical activity.

YouTube, once again, has a plethora of free at-home workouts you can do, many of which require zero equipment or fitness experience at all. Personally, I recommend two days a week of cardio, one day of yoga, 1-2 days of bodyweight or weight/resistance band-lifting, and one day of dynamic stretching. Challenging your body in different ways means keeping your mind alert and flexible, which means you're more receptive to growth and learning.

This also means remaining conscious of the food you're putting into your body. If most of what you eat is junk, most of what you put into the universe is junk. I don't recommend crash diets or radical changes in your eating habits overnight, but I do highly recommend eating filling yet nutritious meals that keep you satiated without leading to lethargy. When we eat foods that properly sustain us, we bring ourselves closer to being true Masterminds.

Be humble

Being a Mastermind does not - I repeat, does NOT - mean you know it all. It doesn't mean you're objectively the best at your craft, you have little or nothing left to learn, or you have the authority to look down upon others who may not be as far along as you. Cockiness and complacency have absolutely no room in a Mastermind's tool book.

To be a humble Mastermind means employing a bit of a mental contradiction: It means working every day toward being the best at your craft while also realizing you're most likely never going to be the best. It means taking the time to learn something new each day while also realizing you're never going to learn it all. It means honing your confidence and having the strength to admit when you don't know the answer to a question. It means taking moments to meditate on the fact that the same energy that created the universe courses through your body while also remembering that you're a flawed human being.

Humility is perhaps the most important tool a Mastermind can have because being humble keeps you grounded; it reminds you that you will always and forever be a student; it showcases the reality that you are not inherently better than the person next to you and that even if you've learned and done so much, there's always room for growth.

Collaborate

It's so important to remember that on the road to success, you don't have to go at it alone. In fact, you can't. No one person is an island, no matter how much we may pride ourselves on our individuality, resourcefulness, and independence. You will always need at least a few people who have your back and who you can learn from as you pursue your goals. Becoming a true Mastermind means connecting with and learning from other Masterminds and potential Masterminds.

Collaboration doesn't always mean working together on a group project (although those are great ways to work toward your goals as well). It can also mean having the strength to reach out to others with questions or to simply bounce ideas off one another. It can mean either connecting with someone you've known for years with similar goals as yours or taking the risk of reaching out to somebody new on LinkedIn you've never met before. The truth is that, more often than not, people are willing to collaborate to help themselves and someone else in the process.

When collaborating with others, ask yourself: What areas of my craft or passion are I not the most knowledgeable about? Who can I connect with to help fill in those gaps? How can I return the favor? Who can I trust as a mentor or an advisor to help me become the best I can be? Once you fully acknowledge and embrace that you don't have to go at it alone, everything ultimately becomes so much easier. It brings you closer to becoming a Mastermind.

Becoming a Mastermind does not come overnight; it takes years of practice and dedication. It means doing everything in your power to become a master of your craft while also staying hungry for knowledge and remembering that you don't have to go at it alone. Finally, it means having the confidence to stay true to yourself, honoring your precious mind and body, and committing yourself to learn and growing every day.

DR. SHANNON WHITTINGTON

About Dr. Shannon Whittington: Shannon (she/her) is a speaker, author, consultant, and clinical nurse educator. Her area of expertise is LGBTQ+ inclusion in the workplace. Whittington has a passion for transgender health where she educates clinicians in how to care for transgender individuals after undergoing gender-affirming surgeries.

Whittington was honored to receive the Quality and Innovation Award from the Home Care Association of New York for her work with the transgender population. She was recently awarded the Notable LGBTQ+ Leaders & Executives award by Crain's New York Business, Daisy Award for Outstanding Nurses, as well as the International Association of Professionals Nurse of the Year award. Whittington is a city and state lobbyist for transgender equality.

To date, Whittington has presented virtually and in person at various organizations and conferences across the nation, delivering extremely well-received presentations. Her forthcoming books include *LGBTQ+: ABC's For Grownups and Kindergarten for Leaders: 9 Essential Tips For Grownup Success.*

Author's Website: *www.linkedin.com/in/ShannonWhittington*
Book Series Website & Author's Bio: *www.The13StepsToRiches.com*

Soraiya Vasanji

SISTERHOODS OR MASTERMINDS OR BOTH

What really is a mastermind?

When a group of people comes together with shared ideas or goals, like wanting to build an online business or master their leadership, these members give and receive ideas, advice, inspiration, motivation, accountability, and honest, constructive feedback. The concept of a mastermind can be applied to a wide range of groups, from formal, professional groups where you have to apply to join, to informal similarly-minded pals meeting together to gab and uplevel. My perspective is that when you bring individuals who share something and are looking for growth, the collective is greater than the sum of its parts. In a mastermind, each member gets to be fully committed, mentally present, and giving and receiving to the collective. There is no playing on the sidelines. There is no playing small; otherwise, this will definitely lead to the collapse of the mastermind. The harmony, collective voice, experiences, and know-how can save someone time, money, energy, emotional collateral, and much more when leaning in on the masterful group. I have experienced some of my biggest ah-has in formal and informal settings, and I have learned that you get what you put in it from a mastermind.

A true, well-functioning mastermind is more than a class, a networking group, a mentoring session, a group coaching session, or friends just getting together. There is a clear intention to advise and share knowledge from experiences—both success and failures, as well as a clear agenda, timeline, accountability, and measures to track growth and movement towards a goal. Members also hold space to deliver feedback and play devil's advocate. We don't know what we don't know, and hearing from people with varied experiences gives us avenues to reflect in ways we may not naturally. All of this comes from wanting the member to succeed because as one member succeeds, the entire mastermind succeeds and breeds more success. While it is true that you can network and share contacts within the mastermind, it has been my experience that the member often goes out of their way to ensure the connection is fruitful in some way for both parties. In networking groups, sometimes people are so focused on themselves and their needs that they are not open nor actually listening to who they are connecting with if they don't appear helpful for their own business at first glance. In a mastermind, people are willing to put their social collateral and network on the line because there is a true buy-in on what value is being created. There are no secret agendas or a mindset of a lose-win situation. A well-run mastermind functions on a win-win mentality; thus, everyone wins in each meeting.

One last note about the mechanics of masterminds is that while there is a facilitator, during discussions, their role can also shift to be someone who receives advice and not only gives it. This then puts everyone on the same level to receive and supply advice and unique perspectives. There is no "taking" energy in this space, only "sharing, up-leveling, giving, and receiving" energy. In a mentoring or coaching group, however, the group's leader typically delivers the teachings to the group. In contrast, in a mastermind, the facilitator can flex and be one with the group.

In a nutshell, a powerful mastermind is a collective group with wide experiences that share wisdom, open up possibilities, deliver feedback and constructive inquiry, foster accountability and action, AND where its members see and accept each other fully.

My two powerful masterminds = The Bombshells & The Sister Tribe

I dedicate this chapter to the active Bombshells and my amazing Sister Tribe, who uses our collective wisdom, joy, and unconditional love to manifest infinite possibilities, committed to our commitments and up-leveling ourselves, creating powerful breakthroughs and BEING what's needed to make ripples that will change the world!

It's hard to say what is the one thing that makes these masterminds powerful and effective, but if I had to summarize it under one category, it would have to be a commitment in that we are all 100% committed to each other which means

- Fully trusting and accepting each other
- Showing up
- Holding space
- BEING open to receiving and giving feedback, even when it can be uncomfortable
- Offering up possibility
- Sharing resources, wisdom, and expertise freely and openly
- Choosing to be in service of each other
- Holding the accountability line
- Mirroring what is working and not working in our leadership
- Being a source and inspiration for choosing love in all ways

I recently endured a lake accident and required emergency surgery for an Anterior Cervical Discectomy and Fusion (ACDF). Which no doubt I was not planning for and threw off everyone's schedule, creating worry, confusion, sadness, and annoyance for my family and friends. While this was all going on, it was in my masterminds that they empathized with what I was experiencing, held a bucket for me to share my frustrations, and most importantly, took the opportunity to reflect and ask thought-provoking questions, which led to my greatest breakthroughs yet.

The Giving and Receiving Game: To be a great "giver," we get to be great "receivers"

Something I talk a lot about in coaching is how to be a "great giver." We also get to be "great receivers." It was this experience of having cervical spine surgery, which was not planned and just decided on a Sunday night and surgery first thing on a Monday morning, that I witnessed my family and friends jump into action to take care of me, my husband, and my daughter. To arrange camp and school pick-ups, meals, and grocery drop-offs, my sister and father dropping everything and flying into Toronto to support us. I couldn't do anything for myself and relied heavily on my husband to support me while my family and friends supported my daughter and household. It was truly surrendering and letting go of how the support looked like and just sitting in a place of abundant gratitude, feeling blessed to have amazing friends like family. To know I am unconditionally loved as I love others unconditionally. My healing was happening from the outside and the inside. When I receive them with open arms, people get to see my appreciation and love for them in a different way. Receiving isn't just about what I am getting but also about what someone can share. What a gift giving and receiving is and how truly it is a gateway to abundance.

- What kind of giver are you?
- What kind of receiver are you?
- What if giving and receiving got to be easy, simple, and free?

Trusting My Inner Voice

Continuing on a breakthrough of understanding the depths of the power of listening and trusting my inner voice, my Bombshell sister and powerful coach, Natalie Gianelli, put me on a stretch to sit in silence and hear and acknowledge this voice. This happened weeks before my lake accident as if the Universe was listening. Learning to accept what my inner wisdom was asking for and actually acting on these wishes were two halves that I got to practice putting together during my recovery. A long time ago, when I lost my twin daughters, I stopped trusting this voice. After many accidents, injuries, arguments, and stubborn feuds, I finally see that events could have turned out differently if I had listened and trusted my inner voice. Through this pain, I finally recognized I was not listening to the voice consistently, and when I didn't hear it, acknowledge it or share it, then less than ideal or rough things surmounted, where If I intervened with my inner intuition and used my voice powerfully a different set of choices may have been presented. I am now artfully practicing daily connection to my intuition and voice. This recovery period shows me just how much my mindset has been working for me and where I have been holding myself small instead of growing and putting myself out there in larger ways!

- How are you using your inner voice powerfully?
- Where do you feel most connected to your inner voice?

I AM A BADASS MINDSET COACH

When you are laid up after cervical neck surgery, smiling, and receiving so much love from family and friends, how can you not be in total bliss and abundance? Well, it seems all my friends were waiting for me to have some kind of meltdown or downward spiral. Sorry to disappoint them, but it never came, and it never will. I have been doing this mindset work for years. I have gone to the depths of physical and emotional pain and can still see the beauty all around me. Is the glass half full or half empty? Wait, there is a glass? Wait, I can see the beauty of a glass holding liquid magic? Oh yes, when you can see the water, the glass, the vessel, and everything as beauty and abundance, there is no space for limiting beliefs and fear to nestle in. During this recovery, I am walking away with letting go of playing small as a coach. Letting thoughts of not being good enough or waiting for one more badge, degree, or certification to say I have made it. I have made it. I am it. All I need is already within me. No one needs to tell me because I know. My masterminds held up the mirrors and asked the reflective questions I was not ready for until now. Each experience leads us to this very moment of what we are ready to learn and see about ourselves.

What are you pretending not to know?

What are you ready to declare?

Now, go find your tribe and join a mastermind.

SORAIYA VASANJI

About Soraiya Vasanji: Soraiya is a Certified Professional Coach (CPC), Energy Leadership Index Master Practitioner (ELI-MP), and has a Master's in Business Administration (MBA) from Kellogg University. She inspires women to be present, not perfect, ditch what doesn't serve them, and create their best messy life now. She loves sharing her wisdom on mindset, the power of language, self-love, self-worth, and leadership principles. She is the founder of the *Mommy Mindset Summit* series, where she interviews experts on topics that interest moms, so they can create a life of authenticity, abundance, and joy—and show their kids how to have it all, too.

Soraiya is married to her soulmate, has a four-year-old daughter, and lives in Toronto, Canada. She is a foodie and a jetsetter, and she loves collecting unique crafting and stationery products!

Author's Website: *www.SoraiyaVasanji.com*
Book Series Website & Author's Bio: *www.The13StepsToRiches.com*

Stacey Ross Cohen

TAP INTO THE COLLECTIVE POWER OF THE MASTERMIND

"No mind is complete by itself. It needs contact and association with other minds to grow and expand."
~ Napoleon Hill, "Think and Grow Rich"

Napoleon Hill popularized the idea of the "Mastermind group" in his book *Think and Grow Rich*. The concept is simple: Two heads are better than one. Collectively pooling resources and knowledge can yield greater success than individuals working separately.

Hill's Mastermind principle was inspired by his many conversations with businessman Andrew Carnegie, who credited his entire success and fortune to his Mastermind group. Likewise, many of the most successful businesses in the world are the product of Masterminds, like Apple's Steve Jobs and Steve Wozniak.

Especially in today's fast-paced world, a Mastermind group is a powerful tool for achieving personal and professional goals. I've been a member of such groups throughout my career and can attest to their impact. Through this powerful network, I've been able to weather business ups and downs, grow my agency, and meet people who have become trusted advisors and friends for life.

MASTERMIND GROUP DEFINED

So, what exactly constitutes a "Mastermind group"? It is commonly believed that Mastermind groups are simply for networking, but that's just one aspect. As you read on, you'll learn they offer so much more.

At its simplest, a mastermind group is a small, select cadre of like-minded individuals who meet regularly (weekly, monthly, or quarterly) to exchange ideas, support each other, share networks, and act as catalysts for growth. Mastermind groups offer a combination of brainstorming, peer accountability, and education to sharpen business and personal skills. Mastermind groups also tend to be goal and success driven. The basic premise is that shared wisdom and experience can shorten the learning curve and accelerate your path to success.

There are mastermind groups for everyone, from CEOs and entrepreneurs to authors and musicians. It's an approach that can be applied to all areas of life, whether you seek to scale a business or inspire creativity.

BENEFITS OF A MASTERMIND GROUP

My 25 years as a business owner have taught me that Mastermind groups are essential to success. And while there's hardly enough room here to list all the benefits they provide, I can name a handful:

Trusted advisors. A Mastermind group is akin to having your own personal board of advisors. Who doesn't want to surround themselves with people who provide trusted guidance and a desire to see them succeed? Expect these advisors to challenge you in a positive way. The group wants you to realize your full potential. Members will provide honest feedback and sometimes the tough love you need.

An expanded network. Masterminds are a great way to expand your network. You'll gain access not just to other members but their networks also. Their network essentially becomes your network, and most members are open to making introductions. Always build and nurture these second-degree relationships. And continually strengthen your relationships with your original fellow members, too. I strive to have a monthly breakfast or lunch with another member.

A sense of community. Mastermind groups aren't just fellow professionals; they're people who care about your success. You're surrounded by people with similar goals, which is very powerful. Other members genuinely have your back and will seek opportunities to help you advance your business or whatever endeavor you're pursuing. For example, I recall one group member undergoing a business partnership break-up and divorce simultaneously. Our group's support was palpable during the meetings, and many of us made certain to check in with the member between sessions to offer support.

Accountability. Accountability is one of the most valuable benefits. It galvanizes members to set and achieve goals. Sharing your plans and goals with others makes us accountable to someone other than ourselves. Having a supportive group of high-achievers to root for us and push us when needed is indispensable. This accountability means you will make better decisions and stay on track.

Business solutions. At some point, we all experience indecision and doubt. Mastermind groups can provide the feedback and support necessary to get back on track. Collective problem-solving gives us both clarity and confidence about difficult decisions. The combined wisdom of multiple trusted advisors overrides a single-minded approach. I have witnessed many stalled businesses in my Mastermind groups experience incredible breakthroughs that changed their businesses' course due to amplified brain power.

Knowledge sharing. Typically, group members have different skill sets and work in various industries. For example, one member may be a marketer in the technology field, while another is an operations professional in the finance field. Due to this diversity, you can learn from others' expertise and insights to enrich your own.

And often, members will have already faced the challenges you're facing now and can give you sage advice.

CHECKING THE BOXES

The benefits of a Mastermind group are now clear, but how do you decide which one to join? Don't fret. I've put together a checklist of things to look for and consider to help select the group that's right for you:

Your goals. What do you hope to achieve by joining a Mastermind group? Be specific and think short and long-term. What's the focus of the group? Is it industry-specific or more general?

Group size. Groups range from eight to virtually thousands (online). It is essential to consider whether you want an intimate setting or a crowded room.

Group types. Mastermind groups come in various shapes and sizes: CEO groups, peer-to-peer communities, retreats, cross-industry groups, and more. Determine what's right for you: a low-key, two-hour weekly meeting in person? Asynchronous interactions on LinkedIn? Or an expensive, quarterly, week-long getaway for brainstorming?

Membership requirements. Some groups require you to have a certain level of experience or minimum annual revenue. For example, CEO groups such as Vistage and Entrepreneur's Organization (EO) require an application and interview process. Members must be business owners, founders, or executives of companies with revenue exceeding $1 million yearly. Be sure to read the fine print before you commit.

Group composition. The best Mastermind groups are carefully curated and composed of individuals with complementary skills and perspectives.

Do members have a similar business model to yours? Are they at a similar stage in their businesses? Does their expertise complement yours, or is it redundant? Diversity is essential.

Group leader. Facilitators are the secret sauce to successful Mastermind groups. The key isn't top-down leadership; it's to create an environment where diverse perspectives are valued and encouraged. In each meeting, the facilitator sets the tone, designs a clear agenda, outlines guidelines, enforces rules, tracks accomplishments, and holds the group accountable.

Level of commitment. Are you all in? For most groups, you must commit fully, meaning always show up and participate. Willingness to give and receive advice, knowledge, and resources is necessary. Come to the table with the mentality of giving more than you get. It is also important to determine if you prefer something short-term or longer-term. A five-year commitment is typical for Mastermind groups, but lengths can vary.

Cost. Make sure you're comfortable with the financial investment required. Some Masterminds charge monthly fees, whereas others are free. Ask questions like: Is there an annual membership fee, and what does it cover? What are the group's cancellation and refund policies? Note that many of these groups allow you to "trial" for free, which I highly recommend.

Ongoing communication. Communication is typically done through email, Slack, Facebook, LinkedIn groups, and Google Docs to provide members with a private space to exchange ideas outside specified meeting times.

In-person vs. virtual meetings. Consider which option would be best for you based on your schedule and location. While online Mastermind groups are often easier to fit into your schedule, nothing will ever replace face-to-face groups. Members tend to be more engaged in live meetings and will be less tempted to multi-task and check their text messages.

A mastermind group is a significant investment; to get the most out of it, you need to enter with the right mindset. Be vulnerable, set goals, build relationships, take advantage of resources, and give before you get.

STACEY ROSS COHEN

About Stacey Ross Cohen: In the world of branding, few experts possess the savvy and instinct of Stacey. An award-winning brand professional who earned her stripes on Madison Avenue and major television networks before launching her own agency, Stacey specializes in cultivating and amplifying brands.

Stacey is CEO of Co-Communications, a marketing agency headquartered in New York. She coaches businesses and individuals across a range of industries — from real estate to healthcare and education — and expertly positions their narratives in fiercely competitive markets.

A TEDx speaker, Stacey is a sought-after keynote at industry conferences and author in the realm of branding, PR, and marketing. She is a contributor at Huffington Post and Thrive Global and has been featured in *Forbes, Entrepreneur, Crain's* and a suite of other media outlets. She holds a B.S. from Syracuse University, MBA from Fordham University and a certificate in Media, Technology and Entertainment from NYU Stern School of Business.

Author's website: *www.StaceyRossCohen.com*
Book Series Website & author's Bio: *www.The13StepsToRiches.com*

Teresa Cundiff

HOW MANY MASTERMINDS ARE YOU IN?

We have the word Mastermind in our regular discourse today because of Napoleon Hill. When he wrote about it, Master Mind was two words, but today we put the words together, and it's not even considered misspelled. A new word has been birthed from the concept. Hill begins his chapter, Power of the Master Mind, by talking about power and how it is "essential for success in the accumulation of money." And yet, I think that today we associate it the other way around: that with money comes power! Hill tells us that power is required to retain money after it's accumulated. Fascinating! And I thought the chapter was just going to tell me how to form a Master Mind of my own. Not exactly!

Proverbs 13:10b says, "But wise men and women listen to each other's counsel," and 13:20a says, "Become wise by walking with the wise." God himself tells us that we should keep the company and take counsel from wise men and women. I think that even if you have never heard the word Mastermind before now that you have probably always felt a synergy when you are with your close friends talking about life, right? Or with work colleagues brainstorming on problem-solving. There is something electric about all the brain power pulling together and looking for an answer. And there is power in that as well!

I have enjoyed many small groups and women's Bible studies throughout my life. My most memorable of those times was when we were posted in England from 1995-97, even though Americans and Brits are two people divided by a common language! LOL! That was always the joke! When they say chips, we think fries, and when we say chips, they think crisps! And we put on our blinkers to pass, and they put on their indicator to overtake! The language things like this go on and on, and we would laugh our silly heads off all the time. It was brilliant (the Brits say this a lot) to get to live there and not just be tourists!

We attended a small church just outside of the main gate of RAF (Royal Air Force) Alconbury, which was attended mostly by Americans, but there were some Brits there as well. Now you have to say R-A-F because saying raff was frowned upon because that sounded too much like riff-raff! Anyway, RAF Alconbury was a US base, and that was where we went to the commissary (USDA beef baby!) and where we got our US mail and did our banking.

My husband was in the Personnel Exchange Program (PEP, because everything must be an acronym!), so we lived on a British post—RAF Brampton, and he worked for the British Army. Somewhere in the US Army, a Brit was working in exchange. Our oldest son, John, went to playgroup the first year and reception at the village school the second year. When in England, we do as the Brits do, so we walked to playgroup like the others on base and rode our bikes to school with everyone else. When Jake, our baby, was old enough, he went twice a week to Creche, which was just two hours long. We were immersed in the culture, and we loved our time there.

We were a very tight community in our church because we were still strangers living in a strange land. That small group of women bonded together like I hadn't really bonded with a group since my sorority days in college. It's the closest thing I can liken to what I feel when plugged into a Mastermind group. We met once a week apart from the church and shared each other's needs, concerns, burdens, and our joys and wins. We would see how we could pool our collective resources to make things work, and there was really nothing we couldn't do when we set our MINDS to a task. And let's face it, we were a bunch of military spouses, and there wasn't anything we couldn't do! LOL!

It also reminds me of another time long ago when I was smart enough to recruit university basketball players to play on the Sigma Chi Little Sisters volleyball team. We won the Intramural Volleyball Championship. We were pulling together in one direction toward a common goal. But the Mastermind does differ in that the whole team pulls together to support the individual in his or her needs/goals. Each team member has differing strengths to help every other member succeed! But you see my point, it's a team effort to see the success of everyone! No one feels isolated, hung out to dry, abandoned, or any of those other words! It's so brilliant! See how I threw in a British reference there? I'm so clever!

As a believer, I claim the promises of God, and I know that I am a blessed person! And I know that the great people I have met in my life and some of the successes I experience are because of the Mastermind groups of which I am a part! And yes, I said groups! It does take more time to be in more than one group, but the benefits are so wonderful! As a member, I learn from the person in the opportunity chair who gets the group's attention and feedback. I am also making connections with everyone and forging friendships. I am getting authoring and networking opportunities and just meeting more phenomenal people! My life is enriched a thousand-fold by my Mastermind groups!

I will confess here that my mindset is not always right. Where can I turn for support? My Mastermind friends! They are not just faces in Zoom boxes! You will find that the longer you are together, the more they become your true friends. Opportunities begin to present themselves for you to meet in person. You do collaboration books together, which leads to book signings. You do summits together. You do business together. You refer clients to each other for products and services. You find that you have built so many wonderful, true, genuine, and lasting relationships over time with some incredible people!

My wish for you, dear reader, is to join a Mastermind group! I can guide you! Please reach out through the info provided at the end of my chapter. You are robbing yourself of such an incredible benefit if you are going it alone. And it's not like you are forced to do anything you don't want to do within the group. But, referring back to what Napoleon Hill said, there is true power in the "third mind" that is formed when two minds come together. He gives a wonderful example about Henry Ford that I encourage you to read for yourself in *Think and Grow Rich*.

Maybe joining a group isn't right for you because you already have a circle that you are happy with! Alrighty then! Formalize it into a Mastermind where you say you're going to meet once a week or twice a month and get more information on what a proper Mastermind looks like. You can do what you want, and there are certifications you can get if you are so inclined. There is so much to gain from the synergy and really nothing to lose from the Mastermind model.

God's word always speaks the truth, and when it says that we will listen to one another's counsel if we are wise, I like to think that I am wise and have sought out wise counsel. Hill states, "a group of brains coordinated (or connected) in a spirit of harmony will provide more thought energy than a single brain." Who wouldn't want more thought energy than a single brain?

So, you're telling yourself that my chapter sounds like a commercial for joining a Mastermind group! And maybe you're right, but in my defense, I always write my chapters as if I were you asking, "What's in this chapter for me?" I hope I have offered you many compelling reasons why you would benefit from being part of such a group. I would also submit that you are probably already part of a group like this that's just called another name. Having that Master Mind working for you can only help you! If you were ever looking for a WIN, you would surely find it here!

TERESA CUNDIFF

About Teresa Cundiff: Teresa hosts an interview digital TV show called *Teresa Talks* on Legrity TV. On the show, she interviews authors who are published and unpublished—and that just means those authors haven't put their books on paper yet. The show provides a platform for authors to have a global reach with their message. *Teresa Talks* is produced by Wordy Nerds Media Inc., of which Cundiff is the CEO.

Cundiff is also a freelance proofreader with the tagline, "I know where the commas go!," Teresa makes her clients' work shine with her knowledge of grammar, punctuation, and sentence structure.

Teresa is a two-time International Best-Selling Contributing Author of *1 Habit for Entrepreneurial Success and 1 Habit to Thrive in a Post-COVID World.* She is also a best-selling contributing author of *The Art of Connection; 365 Days of Networking Quotes,* which has been placed in the Library of Congress. She is a four-time best-selling contributing author to *The 13 Steps to Riches* Series.

Author's Website: *www.TeresaTalksTV.com*
Book Series Website & Author's Bio: *www.The13StepsToRiches.com*

Vera Thomas

GREAT MINDS

Great minds
Small minds
You know the kind
They sit around and gossip
All the time
"Who's doing what?"
"Did it when?"
Not the kind
To call a friend
Average minds
Discussing things
Houses, cars, material gain
GREAT minds
Move the earth
Discussing things Of value of worth
Ideologies of past and present
Realizing dreams
With the mind's consent
Great minds
It takes one to know
These minds
Help ALL minds grow!

~ Vera Thomas

The poem was inspired by an Eleanor Roosevelt quote: "Small minds discuss people, average minds discuss things, GREAT minds discuss ideals." Great minds within a mastermind move the earth!

Napoleon Hill describes a mastermind as "A friendly alliance with one or more persons who will encourage one to follow through with both plan and purpose." My first mastermind experience was during the time when I was asking God why I was born and what is my purpose? There were times I would cry and ask those questions. I attended a mandatory three-day seminar. (I talked about it in the first book in this series). The facilitator was so bubbly, enthusiastic, and full of energy! As the three days unfolded, I felt a stirring in my belly. At the end of the third day, I went up to her and said, "I want to do what you do!" She became my mentor, and thus a mastermind alliance began and a friendship that lasted for many years up until her death. It is because of her that I acquired speaking and presentation skills. She included me in every opportunity to acquire knowledge and experience. I found my purpose; she had a plan! The first thing she suggested was joining Toast Masters. An exceptional training ground. We then attended a two-year twice- monthly training to prepare to join NSA (National Speakers Association). I became certified in several pre-packaged programs, including Zig Ziglar's "See You at the Top." That was over 40 years ago!

In line with Hill's definition, one of my experiences and one of the most effective masterminds was a seven-person mastermind that came together to change the attitudes and mindset of a community with a focus on the criminal justice system, public health, education, and race. The mastermind was comprised of diverse religions, gender, and race. The cohesion among us was second to none. We researched, learned, planned, and implemented on one accord. We met regularly to plan with purpose. We supported each other and made a difference in our community.

When I moved to Kentucky, I was introduced and invited to join an all-women mastermind! Given my purpose for being in Kentucky to care for my sister, who was battling cancer, meeting once a month with women entrepreneurs was just what I needed to remain relevant, gain and share knowledge, network, and support one another. As a result of the mastermind and the networking, there were doors opened that I am sure would not have opened without them.

One of the most valuable masterminds to date is the current experience. The leader and visionary for this 13-book series and the team are authentic and provide the group with training, support, and networking opportunities. It is one of the most rewarding of my life experiences. Of course, some masterminds are not without cost. But the benefits far outweigh the investment in yourself!

In my opinion, what makes a mastermind so powerful is coming together with brilliant minds where knowledge is sustained, networks are established, and collaborations can be rewarding for all involved.

Let us examine some of the benefits of a mastermind.

You will Share Challenges and Successes. As a mastermind member, you will not be on your journey alone. There is an opportunity to share whether business or personal challenges that can impact your business. Members will be supportive and encouraging. As successes are shared, members will be just as optimistic about your success as they are about their own!

You will Get Instant, High-Value Feedback. Meeting regularly as you pursue your dreams and endeavors and having feedback from like-minded professionals and leaders may make your path a little smoother.

You will Get New Ideas and Insights. Like minds where creativity flows and insights are gained. This is an opportunity to think outside the box and beyond your thoughts.

You will Get Help Making Timely Decisions. What a benefit to have great minds being objective to help work through your decision-making process.

You will Collaborate and Synergize. When your efforts are synergistic, the result is a total of the effects that surpasses what one can do on their own. Collaboration, not competition, is a key benefit of masterminds.

You will Improve Your Business by Thinking Bigger. Masterminds can expand your business when great minds explore to help you grow exponentially.

You will Get Ahead of Your Competition. Masterminds provide tools, education, opportunity, and support to enhance your abilities above and beyond your competitors.

There are many more reasons that masterminds are so valuable. Masterminds create lasting connections that go beyond business. Entrepreneurs may have times when they feel alone. Friendships occur that may last well beyond the mastermind experience. One of the things I value about the mastermind I am currently involved with is they give you the time to express and receive feedback. Having one-on-one conversations with members is a gift.

It is an opportunity to challenge yourself. Being in the company of great minds and successful people can only give one the desire to become the best version of themselves.

Masterminds can hold one accountable for their success. Sometimes we allow other things to impact our success and having a group or person hold one accountable can be invaluable.

Getting feedback from others and sharing your feedback and thoughts is one of the benefits of being a mastermind.

Increased confidence is a given when you surround yourself with great minds. Association breeds assimilation, and we become what we are most around. Masterminds are the best company you can keep.

Masterminds can help with clarity and direction. This is especially helpful when so many avenues can be taken. When others can objectively look at your options, it can provide a direction one might not have thought about.

Masterminds provide training from leaders in their field who become part of your existence through the wisdom and knowledge they provide. Therefore, education is very important for masterminds. Remember, you are either green and growing or ripe and rotten. Masterminds are one way to ensure one remains green and always growing along with the great minds of others.

Like anything else, you will get out of a mastermind as much as you put in and more. Feel honored to be among the greats! Do not take it for granted, and know that you are there because you belong. Trust those who God has allowed you to be among. Be thankful for each opportunity to come together to feel love, support, encouragement, and teaching moments.

You may ask, "How do I find a mastermind group?" Some mastermind groups are selective with some criteria. There are paid and free masterminds. When considering joining any, the most important things include your commitment, members feeling valued, there is some structure, and you realize you are there because you belong.

In conclusion, Napoleon Hill is recognized as the founder of the mastermind concept. He recognized and taught how you can accomplish more with and through others than alone. There is power gained through masterminds. Hill stated, "When a group of individuals' brains is coordinated, and functions in Harmony, the increased energy created through that alliance becomes available to every individual brain in the group." If you want to be energized, motivated, encouraged, uplifted, inspired, educated, and increase in business, you want to secure your spot in a mastermind.

VERA THOMAS

About Vera Thomas: Vera Thomas lives in the state of Georgia. She is to date a 6x best-selling author, podcast host, certified transformation coach and family mediator, Classroom Management Advocate/Trainer/Speaker/poet. She works with parents, children, schools, organizations and churches.

Vera's life story directed her towards work with organizations that provided hope and empowerment to people like her to better themselves. It is her goal to help others overcome a circumstance that diminishes and help them to surge ahead with their dreams. Vera graduated "Cum Laude" with a Bachelor in psychology from Walsh University in Canton, OH.

Vera's work as a facilitator for more than three decades and includes developing training programs for youth and adults. Hear her story and think about your own. Vera is available for companies who want to transform their teams or individuals who want to transform their lives.

Author's Website: *www.linktr.ee/VeraThomasInstillingGreatness*
Book Series Website & Author's Bio: *www.The13StepsToRiches.com*

Yuri Choi

POWER OF THE MASTERMIND

As I write this chapter in this villa in Bali, Indonesia, overlooking a beautiful jungle and a private pool, where I am staying for the next few months, I am reminded how synchronistic it is that I am here writing now for a book as an author about masterminds. Life is quite magical that way.

Let me expand. The last time I was here in Bali was a few years ago, shortly after my dad passed away from a brutal battle with cancer. He had battled it for 2.5 years, and my heart was tired. I was in the process of healing from the grief of losing my dad and rebuilding myself as I was moving through a major transition from quitting my corporate job to becoming a full-time entrepreneur. I had a yoga fit apparel line at the time. I was also in the process of building my own coaching practice as a performance coach for high achievers and entrepreneurs.

I share this to preface that I didn't even know I had a dream that I wanted to do anything else at the time with so much going on internally and externally. I didn't think I even had the space and time to dream bigger because I felt like I was already doing a lot and was already dreaming big enough with these new goals and businesses that I was moving forward with. I was already living "enough" outside of my comfort zone.

I found out later, though, that there is a saying that goes, "Bali calls you in and gives you exactly what you need when you need it," to paraphrase. So I didn't know what I needed from Bali on that last trip until it happened.

Originally the vision I had of my trip to Bali back then was a solo trip, but I was invited to join a business mastermind in Bali with other growth-oriented leaders and entrepreneurs, and this community experience sounded intriguing as well. As I had been mostly working as a solopreneur, the idea of spending a week and a half with other like-minded, growth and impact-oriented entrepreneurs in a heavenly place sounded amazing. So I surrendered. I decided to join in on the adventure because the timing felt right. Something told me that this Bali trip would give me exactly what I needed to become the next version of myself.

While I've been to many other masterminds up until that point, this was the first one that was a retreat format in a different continent, where I was living at the time. During one of the mastermind sessions, we were challenged to write down what we wanted to accomplish that we had never dared to say out loud before. I thought to myself, "I really feel like I am already doing everything that I had dreamt about doing. I already quit my corporate job and started my coaching business and fitness apparel line. What else could I possibly mastermind about?"

I remember exactly where we were when I was challenged with this question. We were at this beautiful restaurant overlooking the rice field. We were sitting at a long table with about 10 other growth-oriented people ready to support each other and were traveling and workshopping with me the whole week. It was humid, and I was fighting off some mosquitos that were ready to attack my legs, but nonetheless, it was a peaceful place to reflect and dig deeper, all while feeling safe and embraced by the other mastermind members to open up and have a discussion around this.

What came from that journaling session and the mastermind session was not something I had expected to surface that day. I really thought I'd uncover something I needed to work on for my existing coaching business or my yoga line.

"I want to write a book and become an author."

Whoa. This sentence stared back at me as if asking, "do you remember this dream, Yuri?" And yes, of course, I remembered this dream. Ever since I was little, I have loved writing. I loved to write poetry, I loved to write essays (which was very odd for a grade schooler), and I loved reading. But I had forgotten about it over the years and decades. I did not know this dream was still hiding in the corner of my heart, just waiting for the right moment to come out and confront me like that. Then the second voice started to kick in. Everyone has had the experience with this secondary voice that comes into the conversation uninvited every time you let yourself dream a little bigger. And it sounds something like this... "Wait...Who am I to write a book? Who am I to call myself an aspiring author? Who will actually even benefit from what I have to say? Is what I have to say even valuable enough? What if I make a mistake and I look stupid? No, no, no... this is absolutely not possible for me! This is the worst idea!"

I almost crossed out this sentence about wanting to be an author and writing a book out of my journal because of this voice. It was a loud voice. But then I started to remember. I remember reading this book about a Korean American girl who overcame many obstacles as a first-generation immigrant to the United States when I was young. I was so inspired by her story. Despite the challenges she faced, she ended up going to Harvard University. She became a successful psychologist, which was a dream of hers. I remembered that after reading that book, I told myself that one day I would also write a book to inspire others as she did for me and that I would share my own unique stories in the book to do that. I also wanted to study psychology. Well, the latter, studying psychology, was something I ended up accomplishing in college as it was one of my majors. But what about these other dreams of becoming an author and sharing my stories powerfully? When did I stop dreaming of these as possibilities for myself? And when did I start to bury that dream under layers of "who am I to do that?" imposter syndrome talks?

So I looked up at the long table I was sitting at the mastermind. Everyone seemed to have these internal voices come up as they dreamt, envisioned, and wrote down some of their "scariest" yet "exciting" dreams down as I was. Then it was time for us to actually mastermind and share our visions. One girl shared her dream about leaving her corporate job and starting her own marketing agency. Another shared her dream about starting a charity-related project. Another person shared his dream of starting his own consulting business. It was now my turn.

"I want to become an author and publish a book," I nervously said out loud.

I was secretly scared that they would affirm my biggest fears and say things like, "Who are you to do that? Do you have the right credentials to do that? Do you even know how to get your book published? There are just too many good books and authors out there already. Are you sure you want to do that?" These are the fears that stop most dreams, not just for me but for many out there.

Instead, what I was met with was something completely different. They asked me questions like:

"When do you commit to writing it and publishing the book?"

"Will you hire a coach to help you write and publish the book, or will you do it yourself?" "Would you like me to share the book coach contact with you if you want to hire one?" "Who do you envision this book helping?"

"How will you stay consistent in writing this book in 90 days?" "What is your very next action step toward becoming an author?"

Yes, and I was reminded all over again that this was the power of masterminds. Instead of letting my fears take over the conversation, I was held high in my big dreams and led to new possibilities supporting my dream. I was shaking in excitement and nervousness as my session was completed. Did I just commit to writing my rough draft for my book in 90 days, hiring a coach to help me right when I got back from Bali and publishing my book as soon as possible? How did I just declare this scary goal in front of these 10 people within just 20 minutes?

And so now that I am back in Bali after four years, I can tell you that I am now the author of my book, *Creating Your Own Happiness* (creatingyourownhappiness.com), along with 7 other co- authored books in this *13 Steps to Riches* series. I can call myself a best-selling author. It blows my mind when I really reflect and think about how much has changed since I spoke that dream out loud. And this is why it is so magical to be back here in Bali, now writing about the power of masterminds as this story comes full circle.

Masterminds provide a safe and inspiring place for people to be challenged to dream bigger. Masterminds remind people that when growth-oriented people with similar goals come together, one can collapse time by dreaming big and taking massive action. When one is in an environment where everyone chooses to see you as a ball of infinite potential rather than limitations, the best version of you can emerge and create new possibilities rapidly.

This is why I've continued investing in masterminds and even created Rise Together Mastermind for my clients. Being surrounded by other people who can show up powerfully for one another and allowing yourself to be seen and supported by other amazing humans is beyond incredible. I wonder what buried and dusty dreams can surface and materialize into this world for you, too, if you choose to give it a chance to surface and if you choose to surround yourself with others who see you as the capable, powerful, and unstoppable creator that you are.

YURI CHOI

About Yuri Choi: Yuri is the Founder of Yuri Choi Coaching. Choi is a performance coach for entrepreneurs and high achievers. She helps them create and stay in a powerful, abundant, unstoppable mindset to achieve their goals by helping them gain clarity and understanding, leverage their emotional states, and create empowering habits and language patterns.

She is a speaker, writer, creator, connector, YouTuber, and the author of Creating Your Own Happiness. Choi is passionate about spreading the messages about meditation, power of intention, and creating a powerful mindset to live a fulfilling life. She is also a Habitude Warrior Conference Speaker and emcee, and she is also a designated guest coach for Psych2Go, the largest online mental health magazine and YouTube Channel. Her mission in the world is to inspire people to live leading with L.O.V.E. (which stands for: laughter, oneness, vulnerability, and ease) and to ignite people's souls to live in a world of infinite creative possibilities and abundance.

Author's Website: *www.YuriChoiCoaching.com*
Book Series Website & Author's Bio: *www.The13StepsToRiches.com*

GRAB YOUR COPY OF AN OFFICIAL PUBLICATION
WITH THE ORIGINAL UNEDITED TEXT FROM 1937
BY THE NAPOLEON HILL FOUNDATION!

THE NAPOLEON HILL FOUNDATION
WWW.NAPHILL.ORG

www.ingramcontent.com/pod-product-compliance
Lightning Source LLC
Chambersburg PA
CBHW051617010526
44107CB00043B/1497/J